Whose Story?
Translating the Verbal and the Visual
in Literature for Young Readers

Whose Story?
Translating the Verbal and the Visual
in Literature for Young Readers

Edited by

Maria González Davies and Riitta Oittinen

Cambridge Scholars Publishing

Whose Story? Translating the Verbal and the Visual in Literature for Young Readers,
Edited by Maria González Davies and Riitta Oittinen

This book first published 2008 by

Cambridge Scholars Publishing

15 Angerton Gardens, Newcastle, NE5 2JA, UK

British Library Cataloguing in Publication Data
A catalogue record for this book is available from the British Library

ISBN (10): 1-84718-547-9, ISBN (13): 9781847185471

To Carlos, Juan and Matti

TABLE OF CONTENTS

PART III: Child Images

**PART IV: Teaching and Reading Literature for Young Readers
in Translation**

LIST OF ILLUSTRATIONS

PREFACE

Dear Reader,

The book[1] you're holding in your hands is based on two seminars coordinated by Maria González Davies and led by Riitta Oittinen at the University of Vic, Spain, in 2003 and 2005. At the seminars, doctoral students and researchers from around the world met and discussed issues related to translating, not only the verbal, but also the visual in literature for young readers. The main aims of the discussions were:

- To bring together translation research and practice related to the verbal and visual elements in literature for young readers
- To reflect upon the role of translation as a means to access other communities, and establish or question social roles from early ages
- To explore the challenges posed by the translation of literature for young readers and the translator's decision-making processes
- To describe and share teaching and reading practices related to literature for young readers in translation.

The main focus finally revolved around four questions: Tackling the challenges posed by translating literature for young readers, both picturebooks and books with illustrations, and the range of strategies available to solve specific issues; the special characteristics involved in reading aloud, its emotional dimension, and the sphere it occupies between (the child's future) private and (the child's present public) reading; the interpretation and manipulation of child images; and the role of the translator, publishers and mediators as active or passive agents whose decisions will finally mirror the images projected by the authors of the source books for the readers of the target communities.

The present book, then, is manyfold: it is a set of texts that give voice to all the participants in the seminars. In other words, the book is a meeting point for these different voices and cultures from all over the

[1] This book has been published thanks to the support of the CILCEAL (*Intercultural and Interlinguistic Competence in Language Learning*) research group, University Ramon Llull, Barcelona, Spain.

world, from South Africa to Italy, the Netherlands, Germany, Spain, and Finland. This makes the book very thought-provoking, not just culturewise, but also contentwise.

It is also the purpose of this volume to be professionally-oriented and present examples and cases that underline the interaction between theory and practice. There are many scholars who claim that literature for young readers is not a separate genre, but contains different genres, such as fantasy, poems, plays, picturebooks, fairytales, and novels for young adults. Other debates are centred around readership. For example, whether the demand to pay attention to reading aloud in translation is an issue that comes from a typical feature of literature for young readers, i.e., whether it is aimed at a certain age group.

The issue of age group leads us to pondering on child images, which are based on complex issues such as ideology and manipulation. When translating for young readers or, in fact, when translating any literary work of quality, linguistic and cultural features are closely interwoven in the text and the pictures. This is the crossroads where different communities may converge or diverge due to the deciding authority, either the publisher, author or translator. Who says which books are to be translated and how they are to be translated? Who has the authority to define a translation? For instance, could a re-illustrated text or a book rewritten to become film be considered as an intersemiotic translation or is translation verbal only? What happens when illustrations and cultural references are changed in retellings of fairy tales? Can these crucial aspects serve as a departure point for awareness-raising and discussions on intercultural competence as Maria González-Davies suggests in her chapter?

Bible translation is an issue certainly involving ideological problems. How are we to translate the Bible for children? Is the Bible a religious text only or could it also be defined as a literary work with certain characteristics that should be kept in translation? Bible translation is discussed here from different viewpoints by At Lamprecht and Jackie Du Toit.

The book also deals with the role of the translator. Do translators "just translate" or are they allowed to have a certain agenda? Can translators be active agents in intercultural communication? Do they have a message to convey? Can translators be social activists as Salvador Simó argues in his text on the translation of stories about children who live in conflictive areas of the world?

Moreover, the role of the visual is central in translating books with pictures and picturebooks. The distinction is a valid one, as illustrations play a different role in each case. Riitta Oittinen and Martin B. Fischer put forward some interesting reflections on this issue. It is up to the translator to pay attention to what is said verbally and visually. Translators need both verbal and visual literacy: they need to know how to read illustrations and their interaction with the verbal text: the meanings of colours, patterns and the empty or "silent" spaces in between... They need to know the grammar of the visual, too, such as the symbology or hidden meanings of typography, page margin sizes and all the different ways of combining words and pictures. They also need to be able to recognize different styles and techniques involved in the making of books. Translators also need to be aware of the different ways of recycling characters in books and films.

Translating picturebooks and books with illustrations is highly challenging, partly due to the information given through many different channels: the verbal, the visual, and even the auditive, in accordance with the multimedia dimension of these publications. This may lead the translator to overread the visual and give the future readers of the book too much information. It is very important for the translator to let her/his readers use their imaginations and fill up the hermeneutic gaps by themselves. This goes together with the whole issue of translation strategies and linguistic creativity dealt with specifically by Neus Español, Miquel Pujol, Martin B. Fischer and Maria González-Davies: how the whole question of cultural transplantation or domestication, and exotising or foreignization brings about drastic changes of the reflected child images in different cultures, and how inventiveness and creativity may lead to informed decisions when wordplay and cultural references have to be relayed.

Books with illustrations and picturebooks are usually co-prints (translations into different languages printed by the same printing house), which makes it normally impossible to change any details in the pictures. In this case, the translator may believe there is a need to be overexplicit in her/his verbal text so that it goes together with the illustration. Yet the translator may go overboard and explain more than is necessary.

The aims and discussions mentioned above form part of all the texts, although some of them are forefronted specifically in some, as is usually the case. The topics range from Bible translation, translating the classics, such as Beatrix Potter's tales and fairytales, fantasy worlds for young adults as depicted in Tolkien's *The Lord of the Rings*, or novels such as those by Christine Nöstlinger, stories with a psychological and social function such as the African war tales, and didactic applications that help enhance an awareness of the issues put forward here. In the first part, we start with a general theoretical framework and then we go on to deal with specific translation, linguistic and pragmatic challenges. The third part deals mainly with child images in different communities and in translation and a final chapter deals with ideas on how to exploit these topics with future translators and teachers.

PART I:

GENERAL THEORETICAL FRAMEWORK

CHAPTER ONE

AUDIENCES AND INFLUENCES: MULTISENSORY TRANSLATIONS OF PICTUREBOOKS

RIITTA OITTINEN, UNIVERSITY OF TAMPERE

Abstract

The starting point of my article is translating as rewriting for target-language audiences in target-language contexts. Translating implies change: every time a book is translated, it takes on a new language, a new culture, new readers, and a new point of view. Children's literature, such as picturebooks, has its own special features: children's books are often illustrated and read aloud. Children's books also have a dual audience: children and adults, who read aloud texts for their children.

What is extremely interesting is how the visual information in a story, e.g. picturebook, influences the verbal information and viceversa. In the case of picturebooks, market forces and the concrete ways of printing books also have an influence. Picturebook translations into different languages are often co-printed to save costs, which again has an influence on what kind of stories travel from culture to culture. In books to be co-printed, the pictures usually cannot be changed, which often restricts the translator's choices. These issues will be addressed here and illustrated with picturebooks I have translated myself.

Translating picturebooks: a special field of translation

The relationship of illustrations and texts in words is a very topical issue in the modern world that is so markedly influenced by the visual. Yet the problems of the visual still appeal to few scholars within translation studies, even though translators more and more often have to deal with the visual, like in literary, technical, and media translation.

In several ways, translating picturebooks is a special field of translation: it involves the visual (illustration, cover) and the aural/vocal, when stories are read aloud. Moreover, the situation of using picturebooks involves closeness, the company of the child and the adult who performs the story to the listening child. The Danish scholar Cay Dollerup speaks of a 'narrative contract' between the parties in the read-aloud situation. As he points out, reading aloud is a continuation of the oral tradition, which again makes texts to be read aloud a special field of translation (Dollerup 2003: 82-83, 100).

Translating for an audience also involves a certain image of the audience. The Russian philosopher Mikhail Bakhtin speaks of "super-addressees," who do not exist in the flesh but are authors' assumptions of the future readers of a story (Bakhtin 1979 in Morson and Emerson 1990: 135). The child image of the translator of children's books (and her/his time and society) could also be described as a kind of a "superaddressee": translators direct their words to some kind of a child, which influences the translator's way of addressing the child, such as her/his choice of words (see child image in Oittinen 2000: 41-60).

What is a picturebook?

Before moving any further, I need to define a picturebook, which is no easy task. Several scholars have defined picturebooks as unities formed by words and images, which have a special language of their own. In other words, picture books are iconotexts, with the interaction of two semiotic systems, the verbal and the visual. As iconotexts, picture books and comics or animated films share many features–for example, they are all based on a series of images and have a serial character. Instead of frames, picture books have the turnings of the pages.

The American artist Uri Shulevitz makes a clear separation between picture books and story books: "A *story book* tells the story with words. Although the pictures amplify it, the story can be understood without them. ... In contrast, a true *picture book* tells a story mainly or entirely with pictures. A picture book says in words only what pictures cannot show." (Shulevitz 1985: 15-17).

Yet I find it often much more difficult than the above description to tell a picture book from a story book or an illustrated book. The task gets extremely hard if we consider the postmodern picture book, such as books by Anthony Browne. As David Lewis points out in his *Reading Contemporary Picturebooks. Picturing Text* (2001), what is distinctive of postmodern picture books is their diversity: canons and boundaries have faded, and there is "mixing of forms ... parody and pastiche." (see Lewis 2001: 90).

The complexity of the picturebook makes me reluctant to compare picture books with story books and I'd rather use the term "picturebook" in the sense of Perry Nodelman: a picture book is the "province of the young child"; picturebook also "uses many codes, styles, and textual devices" and "frequently pushes at the borders of convention." (Nodelman 1999: 69-80). There is one more thing I would like to add to the above: a picturebook is a polyphonic form of art. In other words, it is an art form with many different voices to be heard and seen. In picturebooks we can hear the voices of the author, the illustrator, the translator, and the different readers, children and adults.

Reading and translating picturebooks as a semiotic process

Translators always start their work as readers. Translators of picture books start their work as readers of both words and illustrations. Mikhail Bakhtin speaks of the dialogics of all human understanding. A reading experience is dialogic and consists not only of the text but also of the different writers, readers, and contexts, and the past, present and future. Human words are always born in a dialogue (Bakhtin 1990: 426-427).

Bakhtin stresses the "unfinalizability" of all reading and understanding. And he makes a clear distinction between "the given" and "the created." "The given" is "the 'material,' the resources, with which we speak and act" (Bakhtin 1987: 166), that is, concrete words and illustrations. "The given" also comprises language, culture, and the human being's background. And yet no book, no original or translation, is only a "product" of what is given, but something new is created in the process of understanding and interpretation.

Dialogue is not far removed from what Bakhtin calls heteroglossia: "At any given time, in any given place, there will be a set of conditions – social, historical, meteorological, physiological – that will ensure that a word uttered in that place and at that time will have a meaning different than it would have under any other conditions." (Bakhtin 1990: 428). Words are heteroglot: they are situated in time and place and born between the own (like the source culture) and the alien (like the target culture). If we change one tiny item in the set of conditions, the whole situation is changed. Illustrations are also part of the context of the words and the other way around. If we change the pictures or the words, the set of conditions are changed, too. Detached from its context, a word or a picture is different. For instance, when I placed a picture from Maurice Sendak's *Where the Wild Things Are* on my kitchen wall, the picture became detached from its context and took on different meanings from the meanings the picture had as a page opening in the book.

Translating the verbal and the visual of picture books may also be understood as a semiotic process. Like Bakhtin, the American semiotician Charles Sanders Peirce describes semiosis as an endless process of interpretation and human cognition, involving signs. (Peirce 1932: 229) From the viewpoint of picture books, a word, an image, a page and even a whole book may be seen as signs. Everything in a book is of importance. Every detail carries meanings, which are to be interpreted by the translator. There are also many different visual and cultural signs that translators need to be aware of, such as, for instance, the reading direction and the symbolism of colors (e.g., ritual colours).

Peirce introduces three orders of signs: icon, index, and symbol. Icon is a sign of likeness; like a photograph, it resembles the thing it is referring to. Index is something that is in a causal relationship to its referent, like smoke implying fire. Symbol is an artificial sign: words are symbols referring to things in the real world just by agreement. There is no logical connection between meaning and the symbol itself, but it's something we have to learn. All the different signs can be found in a picture book. A picture is an icon; a picture of a girl resembles a real girl. A word in a picture book is a symbol based on agreement, and there is an indexical relationship between the words and the images. It is this relationship that influences the translator's choice of words and her/his idea of the whole book. In semiotic terms, translating picture books is intersemiotic translation (Peirce 2001: 415-426).

Fish in the forest: meeting with texts

Peirce also discusses the three phases of meeting with texts: Firstness, Secondness, and Thirdness, which can also be applied to picturebook translation. At the first encounter with the text, we just feel it, without any analysis whatsoever. Like with the feeling of heat and cold, we just take the text in. At the second stage, secondness, we start analyzing what we have felt, pondering on things. At the third stage, we start thinking of the future, translating the text for an audience (Peirce 2001: 415-421).

In the following I'm applying Peirce's views about semiosis and the three phases to my Finnish translation of Hugh Lupton and Niamh Sharkey's collection of fairy tales *Tales of Wisdom & Wonder*. As an example, I chose the Russian folk tale "Fish in the Forest". In the first part,

Firstness, I tell the story as I read it and describe my first impressions of the visual in the story. In the second part, Secondness, I take a closer look at the verbal and the visual: In which ways do the verbal and the visual interact? What is told in words and what in images? What should I, as a translator, take into consideration? What kind of problems do I have with the visual? In the third section, Thirdness, I briefly describe my strategies and solutions, based on my first and second impressions (See Oittinen 2004: 158-178 and forthcoming).

Firstness

The story tells us about a farmer and his wife, who could never keep a secret. One day, when digging turnips in the field, the farmer found an old chest full of gold. He was happy but also worried: how could he keep this secret from his wife? The Tzar was very greedy and would not hesitate to take their gold if he found out about it. So, on the following night, the man tried to hide the treasure from his wife, but in vain: the wife woke up and saw the sparkling treasure. Then the man thought and thought and in the end he had an idea. He got out of bed early in the morning and bought some trout, buns, and sausages. Then he hurried into the forest and scattered the fish on the ground, set the buns among the branches of the trees, and hooked the fish on the end of a fishing line. On the following morning they woke up and the man asked the wife to go with him to the woods. The wife followed and saw all the amazing things in the forest: fish among the grass, buns on the trees, and sausages on the fishing line. But then the Tzar found out about the treasure and summoned the man and his wife. And the wife told the Tzar everything about the treasure. But when she told the Tzar that it all happened when they, on the following day, had seen fish on the ground, buns on the trees and sausages on the fishing line, the Tzar got very angry and said that he didn't believe a word of what the woman had said. In this way the farmer and his wife kept their gold and lived happily ever after.

The story is rhythmic and easy to read aloud; it is full of humor and repetition (many of the sentences start with "and"). There are not many details in the illustrations, and yet the images of the man and the woman are very much alive. The man is wearing big trousers; the woman wears a big apron. The Tzar is said to be the King, but he looks more like the Tzar of Russia than any king. And in Russia, they didn't have any kings.

The story starts with a picture of the man standing under the moon. At the bottom of the page, like on every page, there is a row of fish. On the right-hand page of the first opening, there are the man's two big feet and one turnip that has been pulled out of the ground.

On the second opening, pages 3 and 4, the man is carrying a heavy chest and the woman is looking out of the window. When I took a better look at the picture though, I realized that it wasn't any window but a picture of the woman. Yet it gives the impression that the man is looking at the woman and feeling very guilty indeed. The woman is looking back and their looks meet. On the right side of the opening, page 4, there are Russian-style houses decorated with pictures of a fish, a bun, and a sausage.

On the third opening, there is only one big picture that covers the upper part of both of the pages. On the left, the woman is standing with raised hands and looks very astonished. I cannot see her mouth but the position of the hands gives her a surprised look. The man is standing on the right and he follows the woman's reactions very carefully. There are fish and buns all over the picture.

On the fourth opening, on the left, there is only the row of fish at the bottom. On the right hand, there is a full-page picture of the castle, the woman, and a hen that looks very unhappy about the obvious fact that the woman is taking her eggs to the market. The colour in this page is much heavier than anywhere else: it is dark reddish brown. In the background, the illustrator has drawn Russian letters and words.

On the fifth opening, on the left, there is the Tzar: he looks very grim, very powerful and very greedy. He's very big but has very tiny eyes. He looks down on the woman who is standing on the right wearing rabbit ears. At the background of the woman, I discern three distant figures waving their hands.

Secondness

According to Shulevitz, the book is probably not quite a picture book. On the other hand, without the illustrations, the story would be lacking a lot of information. And the mood would certainly not be the same.

The illustrator has stylized the characters: their eyes are drawn as small dots. The man is also identified with his big trousers–as being the man in the house; the woman with her big apron, as being a woman and taking care of the household. It seems that the illustrator has rather wanted to underline the roles of the characters and their moods than their actual features. (Of course, the same detail is shown in the story told in words: the man and the woman don't have any names.) Doing so, the illustrator has raised the story to a more general level. Now the story is as much a story about a certain farmer and a certain wife as it is a story about the great lion (the Tzar) and the tiny little mouse (the farmer): the mouse is wise enough to beat the powerful lion. On the other hand, it is interesting that the man is actually afraid of the woman's reactions. In the end, it is hard to tell who is deceiving who.

The most powerful element in the illustrations is humor. The characters are easy to like (except for the Tzar) and the story is very entertaining. For the most part, the colors are light and dim, and yet the illustrations have a powerful influence on the story told in words. As a whole, the images together with the words gave me an idea of the tone of my language: the story should be readable, even singable on the aloud-reader's tongue.

The pictures and words take turns. Sometimes the author gives many details and the illustrator none. This is the case with the rusty chest, which is drawn as a mere square but explicitly described with words. On the other hand, when the woman sees the man's setting of fish, buns, and sausages, the author does not say how the man feels about the woman's reaction. Yet the illustrator has drawn the man with circled eyes, which makes him look very wary and attentive indeed.

Sometimes the illustrator has combined things happening at different times in the story. On the second opening, the man is carrying the chest and the woman is upstairs looking at the man. In the story told in words, the woman runs first downstairs and only then sees the man and the chest. There are also other paradoxes in the story. For example, the story clearly takes place in Russia, but the author speaks of the king. Throughout the illustrations, there are references to Russian culture.

There is also one picture, which makes the translator's task difficult. The picture of the woman wearing rabbit's ears as well as the words referring to the picture: "Mad as a March hare!" clearly refer to Lewis Carroll's "Alice." Yet, in the Finnish language, we don't have any similar phrases about rabbits. Moreover, the story of "Alice" is not quite as well known to Finnish readers, which means that it may be questionable to use a reference to Carroll's "Alice." Anyway, I decided to use the phrase and let the readers make their own conclusions.

On the last opening of the story, the composition, the way the illustrator has situated the Tzar and the woman, tell about their status in society: the Tzar is high up on the left and looking down on the woman. The woman looks tiny and humble on the bottom of right hand page and doesn't dare to look at the Tzar. The people at the background of the picture look as if they were laughing at the woman's stupidity.

Thirdness

After considering my first impressions of the book, I started forming an entity and making the illustrations and my Finnish-language interact. In the core of my iconotext was the fact that the story is clearly a folktale and meant to be read aloud. I added repetition and avoided condensed language; I also read my text aloud several times.

The problem of the March Hare was not as hard to solve as I first feared. I believe that my Finnish readers who recognize the intertextual reference are happy with my solution. And those who do not recognize the rabbit take my words as referring to the picture depicting the woman with rabbit ears. As to the Tzar, I decided to call him the Tzar (tsaari) in Finnish, too, as that is the term we use for former Russian rulers. Moreover, in this way the translation goes nicely together with the illustration.

On the other hand, the illustrations helped me in many ways, especially when forming my translation strategy. The alternating of the words and images made me think of how much I could reveal at certain points of the story. Sometimes it was very hard, especially at those points when the illustrator shows in one picture two things taking place at different times.

I believe I finally managed to create an entity, a new iconotext, which is both entertaining and easy to read aloud. Yet I know that my semiosis is only one possible among many other possible semioses.

Translating picturebooks: coherence and effect

When reading the visual and interpreting images, there are a number of conventions we need to know. John Spink, the American scholar on children's books, has studied children as viewers of illustrations. According to Spink, we need to be aware of conventions like "scaling down" (a picture is smaller than the thing in itself), "indicating three-dimensional objects in a two-dimensional medium", and "indicating colour in monochrome". For example, when we see a picture of a landscape, we can imagine the colors and the depth in the picture.

Yet the visual appearance of a book includes not only the illustrations, but also the actual print, the shape and style of letters and headings, composition, and picture sequence. Even the elements of the layout and typography can be strictly culture-bound. In *Translating for Children* I present an example of the Finnish author and illustrator Tove Jansson's picture books. In my example, such a seemingly tiny detail as the shape of letters can be considered as a translation problem. In the Swedish-language original *Vem skall trösta knyttet?* (1960, *Who Will Comfort Toffle?* 1991) and its Finnish-language version *Kuka lohduttaisi nyytiä?* (1970) the words are written in cursive and look somehow "hand-written." They seem to bring "closeness" to the reading situation and they complement the stylized paper-cut technique used in the illustrations.

Yet, for some reason, the publisher of the English and German versions decided to use ordinary typeface, which emphasizes the linearity of the text blocks. In this way, the text in words is more clearly separated from the illustrations, and there is no rhythmic fluctuation of hard and soft lines any more.

This detail of handwriting is more significant than it may seem on first sight. As many studies on Jansson's art show, she typically gives rhythm to her narration by counterpointing opposites like safety and danger. And this is seen in her illustrations as well. The same rhythm is repeated in the roundness of the handwriting and the hard squares of the text blocks; every detail is part of the whole. As to the readability of the cursive writing, I have read this book (in Finnish) aloud to children of all ages, and the hand-written text has been a source of delight to both the reader and the children listening and looking on. On the other hand, with different readers in different cultures the situations are different, too. For instance, unlike in Finland, in American schools children might find cursive writing even difficult to read.

Whatever the translator decides to do in individual situations, she needs to be aware of the visual effect on different text types. As Joseph Schwarcz points out, in picture books, letters and words may have various tasks and forms. For instance, letters may be signs of loud or soft sounds by growing bigger or smaller. For example, it is very important to pay attention to how – and from which angle – the characters are looking at each other. Even placing one figure higher than the other may tell of a higher status of the character.

A picture book is a combination of the verbal (silent and aloud reading), the visual, and also the effects like sound bulbs or movement lines. All these details add to the contents of the story. As a whole, the visual appearance of a book always includes not only the illustrations but also the actual print, the shape and style of letters and headings, composition, and picture sequence. The American scholar Rudolph Arnheim (1974) speaks of different kinds of movement: not only actual, physical movement, but also other kinds of motion. Either the object moves or the mind of the viewer moves. For instance, if we take a picture of a dancer, we have a certain memory of what a dancer in motion looks like. We are fooled into seeing motion where there is none and we can add the missing details with our own imaginations.

Many scholars suggest a division of four functions of the visual. An illustrated text may be based more on pictures than on words, or the other way around; there may also be collaboration of the verbal and the visual; or the visual may tell quite a different story than the verbal. In other words, illustrations affect the reading experience through congruency and deviation. Deviation may also be called irony: when the visual is telling something very different from what the words are doing, the reader stops believing in what she/he is being told and starts putting words and images in quotation marks.

We might also say that illustrations both domesticate and foreignize. Illustrations may bring the text closer to the story told in words. By means of domestication, keeping close to the text in words, they add to the smooth entity. On the other hand, by telling a different story than the text in writing, illustrations may also foreignize: in this way they bring along intrusion of something foreign, something unclear, something maybe difficult to understand. While domesticating, translators need to pay special attention to the visual. If, for instance, a story is situated in Paris, France, and the illustrator shows the Eiffel tower and other landmarks of the city, the end result may be strange, if, in the Finnish translation, the story is situated in Helsinki, Finland.

Translator's choices and strategies

Translators interact with illustrations in many ways. On the one hand, translators try to match the text in words and the illustration; on the other, translators have – either consciously or unconsciously – internalized the images from their reading of the words and illustrations.

When solving the problem of the verbal and visual, translators may choose different strategies. The Finnish translation scholar Andrew Chesterman, following the Polysystem Theory, has pointed out that translators' strategies are governed by different norms, which promote certain values and ethics (see, e.g., Chesterman in Oittinen et al. 2004: 341-348). Norms place restrictions on the translator but they also give her/him freedom.

There are several strategies that translators may use, such as addition and omission. Translators may, for example, add comments like footnotes to explain and clarify some culturally specific details. At best, this helps the reader to understand and enjoy the book better; at worst, the translator may destroy the pleasure of the reading experience. In picturebooks, footnotes are probably not suitable, unless the very idea of the book is to play with book conventions (see, e.g., Scieszka et al. 1992).

Moreover, translators also need the ability to recognize the gaps left in the text by the author and the illustrator. Sometimes translators may feel tempted to explain the story told in words on the basis of what they see in the illustration. However, this may change the indexical relationship of the verbal and the visual altogether. This may result in dull texts, explaining too much, and giving no room for the reader's own interpretation. This happened to the American edition of Michel Gay's *Papa Vroum* (*Nightride*) and the first German translation of John Burningham's *Granpa* (*Mein Opa und ich*) (see Emer O'Sullivan in Lathey (ed.) 2007: 113-121).

The Jordanian scholar Jehan Zitawi (2004) also deals with visual manipulation, which is common in translating comics from English into the Arabic, especially in the Persian Gulf area, and rather uncommon in Europe and North America. This is probably partly due to the use of co-prints, where translations into different languages are printed at the same time. Yet sometimes illustrations may be censored, too, like in one scene in the Finnish picture book artist Kristiina Louhi's *Aino* series (1985), where the little girl Aino's little brother is going out and about to get dressed. On the Finnish original book cover the little boy is running in the snow stark naked, except for a tiny cap on his head. The Finnish readers find the cover only funny, a prank by a very little boy, but Methuen, the British publisher of the translation, found the cover obscene and wanted the artist to change it. In the end, in the British version (1987), the little boy is fully dressed (see Louhi in Oittinen 2004: 116-117).

Whichever strategy the translator chooses, and for whatever reason, illustrations may help her/him in many ways: they show the time and place where the story is situated. They also show the looks and the relations of the characters in the story. As a whole, illustrations give all kinds of hints to the reader. Sometimes the text in words does not give this kind of information, and yet it can be found in the pictures (see above the "Fish in the Forest").

Illustrations also help by showing how things look like exactly. With the knowledge about the details, it is easier for the translator to describe what the characters do and how they sound. If, for instance, the illustrator shows how many petticoats a princess has while she is running, it is easier for the translator to visualize the situation and describe what kind of sounds she makes. When I and a group of students translated Lee Kingman's *The Secret Journey of the Silver Reindeer,* Lynd Ward's illustrations were of great help whcn making the decision of which verb to use when describing the sound of the reindeer's hooves, because the illustrator showed the hard snow covering the earth.

Illustrations may also create great problems for translators, because, due to co-prints, usually pictures cannot be altered. At first the translations into different languages are printed at the same time by an international publisher; then the books are released by the national publishers. Taking co-prints also influences the book publishing business on a more general level – and not always in a positive way. The practice of taking co-prints implies that several countries want to have the same book(s) translated and that only such books are chosen that "travel" easily from one culture and language to another.

Sometimes pictures are heavy-weight opponents, like when I translated two books by the South African author-illustrator Niki Daly. The first story tells about a little black South African Zulu girl Jamela living with her mother. In one of the scenes of the book *Jamela's Dress* (1999) I encountered with a problem concerning the visual. In one scene, the little girl Jamela and her mother are playing games and singing while waiting for a beautiful fabric to get dry. The fabric was to become the mother's dress for a wedding party. In the scene Jamela asks her mother: "Lets' do teapots, Mama!" and teaches her mother how to do "a little song about a teapot with a spout. They dipped and tipped and the tea poured out." In the Finnish culture we don't have anything quite similar, so I decided to read the illustration more closely and try to find a song game matching with the body and hand movements shown in the illustration. After a long hunt, I found the Finnish song "Aamulla herätys, sängystä pois", which tells about what people do in the morning when they wake up. In the end, the solution seems successful, as the tune is international ("Lou, Lou, Skip to My Lou") and the way the song is played in Finland is very close to Jamela and her mother's hand and body movements.

Another example of how the illustrator's solutions influence the translator's work is *To Every Thing There Is a Season* (1998) by the American artists Leo and Diane Dillon, which I translated quite recently. The passages in the book are from the Book of Ecclesiastes, the King James version of the *Bible*. On every page opening there is one line of the book with an illustration depicting different cultures and different periods of time. After reading the book a few times, I decided to use an existing translation: the newest Finnish translation of the *Bible* from 1992. However, my decision proved to be problematic in a passage that goes like this: "A time to embrace, and a time to refrain from embracing." The translators of the 1992 Finnish version had a different point of view than the translators of the King James version. The 1992 version reads: "aika on syleillä ja aika olla erossa," which can be rendered into English as: "Time to embrace and time to be separated." Now there was an unwanted contradiction of the story told by the verbal and the story told by the visual. On the left-hand page, the family are in a private home, embracing and leading a cosy family life. On the right-hand page, the family are working together; they are probably tradespeople as there are coins and a pair of scales on the table. The family are not embracing but they are still together and certainly not separated.

To solve the problem, I decided, in this part of the text, to use an older Finnish translation from 1933, where the translator's solution is very close to the King James version: "Aika on syleillä ja aika olla syleilemättä." In English: "A time to embrace and a time to refrain from embracing." Elsewhere in my translation I leaned on the newer 1992 version. There are forewords in the book, so it was easy for me to add a comment on my solution, which was, in its entirety, based on the iconotext, the indexical relationship of the words and the illustration.

The authors of picturebooks also give visual hints to readers through punctuation and sentence structure. Through punctuation, like using commas and full stops, as well as sentence and word length, the reader is given subtle instructions on when to stop and when to make haste. At periods and commas, the aloud-reader may stop to breathe in. In the case of books to be read aloud, the translator is supposed to make the aloud-reader's task as easy as possible. The text to be read aloud must roll on the aloud-reader's tongue; the verbal text also needs to collaborate with the visual and the turnings of the pages.

Sometimes it is clearly mentioned that the book is supposed to be read aloud, like in Hugh Lupton and Sophie Fatus's *The Story Tree. Tales to Read Aloud* (1998). Lupton's verbal text is full of repetition, alliteration, and side addresses to the reader/listener. The story "The Sweetest Song" begins like this:

> **ONCE UPON A TIME Little Daughter was picking flowers. Once upon a time Little Daughter was picking flowers** on the far side of the fence. **Her papa had told her not to. Her mama had told her not to.** But her papa and mama weren't watching and Little Daughter had seen a beautiful yellow flower nodding in the breeze just beyond the fence. (My bolding)

The illustrator has a similar repetitive style, and the main characters, the Little Daughter and the wolf, simultaneously appear several times on each page. The Finnish translation (2001) goes like this:

OLIPA KERRAN Pieni Tytär, joka poimi kukkia. Olipa kerran Pieni Tytär, joka poimi kukkia liki aitaa kaukana kotitalostaan. Isä oli häntä kieltänyt. Ja äiti oli häntä kieltänyt. Mutta isä ja äiti eivät aina ehtineet katsoa Pienen Tyttären perään, ja tytär oli juuri nähnyt kauniin keltaisen kukan, joka nyökytteli lempeässä tuulessa aivan aidan toisella puolella. (My bolding)

Even without competence in the Finnish language, it is easy to see that the author's message certainly influenced the rhythm, punctuation, and overall style of my translation.

Some final thoughts

Translators of picture books translate whole situations including the words, the illustration, and the whole (imagined) reading-aloud situation. When reading picturebooks, readers participate in a dialogue between themselves and the story told by the author and the illustrator with words and pictures. Yet the verbal, the visual, and their dialectical and indexical relationship are also part of a greater whole: the original work and its translations and the various individual readers in different cultures.

Translating picture books may also be compared with translation for the theater. As in drama translation, translators of picture books need to pay attention to the readability of the verbal text: the text is "performed" for the child and it must flow while being read. In addition, the illustrations are a kind of set design for the text: as in the theater, they have an effect on the audience. Like theater translation, picture book translation is a stage for a multitude of voices.

Works cited

Arnheim, Rudolph. *Art and Visual Perception. A Psychology of the Creative Eye.* Berkeley and Los Angeles: University of California Press, 1974.

Bakhtin, Mikhail. *Problems of Dostoyevsky's Poetics.* English translation by Caryl Emerson and Michael Holquist. Austin: University of Texas Press, 1987.

—. *The Dialogic Imagination. Four Essays.* English translation by Caryl Emerson ja Michael Holquist. Austin: University of Texas Press, 1990.

Carroll, Lewis. *Liisan seikkailut ihmemaassa.* Illustration by John Tenniel. Finnish translation by Kirsi Kunnas and Eeva-Liisa Manner. Jyväskylä: Gummerus, 1972.

——. *Alice's Adventures in Wonderland and Through the Looking-Glass.*
Illustration by John Tenniel. New York: Bantam Books, 1981 (1865).

Chesterman, Andrew. "Kääntäminen teoriana" In *Alussa oli käännös*,
edited by Riitta Oittinen and Pirjo Mäkinen, Tampere: Tampere
University Press, 2004.

Daly, Niki. *Jamela's Dress.* London: Frances Lincoln, 1999.

——. *Jamelan leninki.* Finnish translation by Riitta Oittinen. Kärkölä: Pieni
Karhu, 2001.

Dillon, Leo and Diane. *To Every Thing There Is a Season.* New York: The
Blue Skye Press, 1998.

——. (Unpublished Manuscript) Finnish translation by Riitta Oittinen.

Dollerup, Cay. "Translation for Reading Aloud" In *Translation for
Children /Traduction pour les enfants. Meta*, edited by Riitta Oittinen,
no. 48, nos 1–2, mai 2003.

Jansson, Tove. *Vem skall trösta knyttet? (Who Will Comfort Toffle?* 1991),
Helsinki, WSOY, 1960.

——. *Kuka lohduttaisi nyytiä?* (Finnish translation by Kirsti Kunnas),
Ponvoo: WSOY, 1970.

Lewis, David. *Reading Contemporary Picturebooks. Picturing Text.*
London and New York: Routledge, 2001.

Louhi, Kristiina. *Aino ja pakkasen poika.* Espoo: Weilin and Göös, 1985.

——. *Annie and the New Baby.* Engl. David Ross. London: Methuen
Children's Books, 1987.

Lupton, Hugh. *Tales of Wisdom & Wonder.* Illustration by Niamh
Sharkey. Bath: Barefoot Books, 1998.

——. *Ihmesatuja eri maista.* Illustration by Niamh Sharkey. Finnish
translation by Riitta Oittinen. Kärkölä: Pieni Karhu, 2001.

——. *The Story Tree. Tales to Read Aloud.* Illustration by Sophie Fatus.
Bath: Barefoot Books, 2001.

Lupton, Hugh. *Tarinatie. Tarinoita silmälle ja korvalle. Illustration by*
Sophie Fatus. Finnish translation by Riitta Oittinen. Kärkölä: Pieni
Karhu, 2002.

Morson, Gary Saul and Caryl Emerson. *Mikhail Bakhtin: The Creation of
a Prosaics.* Stanford: Stanford University Press, 1990.

Nodelman, Perry. "Decoding the Images: Illustration and Picture Books"
Hunt, Peter (ed.) *Understanding Children's Literature,* 69-80. London
and New York: Routledge, 1999.

Oittinen, Riitta. *Translating for Children.* London and New York:
Garland, 2000.

——. *Kuvakirja kääntäjän kädessä.* Helsinki: Lasten Keskus, 2004.

—. *Translating Picturebooks* (working title) Clevedon, Buffalo, Toronto: Multilingual Matters, forthcoming.

O'Sullivan, Emer. "Translating Pictures" In *The Translation of Children's Literature. A Reader*, edited by Gillian Lathey, 113-121. Clevedon, Buffalo, Toronto: Multilingual Matters, 2007.

Peirce, Charles S. Collected Papers by Charles Sanders Peirce. Cambridge and London: Harvard University Press, 1932.

—. *Johdatus tieteen logiikkaan ja muita kirjoituksia*. Finnish translation by Markus Lång. Tampere: Vastapaino, 2001.

Raamattu (the Bible, Finnish translation) 1933.

—. (the Bible, Finnish translation) 1992.

Schwarcz, Joseph H. 1982 *Ways of the Illustrator. Visual Communication in Children's Literature*. Chicago: American Library Association.

Scieszka, Jon. *The Stinky Cheeseman and Other Fairly Stupid Tales*. Kuv. Lane Smith. New York: Viking, Penguin Group, 1992.

Sendak, Maurice. *Where the Wild Things Are*. USA: Harper & Row, 1963.

Shulevitz, Uri. *Writing with Pictures. How to Write and Illustrate Children's Books*. New York: Watson-Guptill Publications, 1985.

Spink, John. *Children as Readers. A Study*. London: Clive Bingley, Library Association Publishing Limited, 1990.

The Holy Bible. King James Version, Canada: World Bible Publishers, (No year of publication).

Zitawi, Jehan. *The Translation of Disney Comics in the Arab World: A Pragmatic Perspective*. Manchester: The University of Manchester, School of Modern Languages, CTIS, 2004.

CHAPTER TWO

THE COGNITIVE UNCONSCIOUSNESS
IN THE TRANSLATION AND ILLUSTRATION
FOR CHILDREN–AN EMBODIED CHALLENGE

AT LAMPRECHT, NORTH-WEST UNIVERSITY,
POTCHEFSTROOM, SOUTH AFRICA

Introduction

In traditional approaches to the translation of the verbal and the visual in children's literature (with specific reference to ancient religious texts), the unconscious linguistic operations of the human mind were neglected in favour of an effortless literal interpretative conversion of text into illustration. The effect was sometimes unusual visual imagery or even fiction, as the illustration of *Elijah's ascension to heaven in a storm, in a chariot of fire, and pulled by horses of fire*[1] found in children's Bibles, shows. The study on which this section is based challenged this current translation processes by recognising the cognitive unconsciousness, enabling the "connection" of the illustration in the translated text to the "image" in the symbolic function of language.

Language, as an expresser of our minds, is used in creative ways. Evidence for such creativity is the semantic structure of our expressive thoughts about certain abstract concepts within a concrete symbolic assembly. Take for example the concrete expression in African-American spiritual music *"he crossed over Jordan"*, for the "special" idiomatic meaning of "he died". The meaning of this concrete phrase is not mere sum of its constituent parts, but is interpreted as a whole single unit: a construction. This construction is presumably learned and is stored in a mental "box", while the context behind this learned symbol has most likely long been forgotten. Hence, in order to communicate, people use great creativity while obeying many complicated rules. As such, even in ancient religious documents, linguistic operations leave traces behind since "every word the speaker uses is associated in his mind with a certain mental representation" (Putnam 1988: 19). In translating and illustrating ancient religious texts, it is therefore the present-day interpreter's task to investigate these traces to do justice to the intended meaning. The following three notions about language may be used as an appropriate framework for the determination of meaning in an extra-experiential cultural context:

- a symbolic assembly is a form-meaning pairing, thus consisting of an image (Evans and Green 2006: 7);
- images are representations of specific, embodied[2] experiences (Fillmore 1977: 73-75); and
- the inter-dependency of the symbolic assembly relies on the pragmatic information or context in which the utterance occurs (Evans and Green 2006: 12).

Meaning is therefore grounded in the shared human experience of bodily and cultural existence, based on structures of imagination (and filtered by perception). Thus, human bodies and culture give us an experiential basis for understanding a wealth of concepts, such as death.

Humans have effective abilities for the construction of meaning. Amongst others are language and illustrations (or art) two of the most elaborate forms. Illustrations for children, although constructivist in nature, should be regarded as a specific kind of cognitive engineering (Donald 2006: 4). The operation of imagination, which is mostly unconscious, is at the heart of even the simplest possible meaning (Donald 2006: 4). Usually, the expressive source (such as death) is endowed with a concrete mode of sensory presence.

Since the approach used in translating and illustrating ancient religious literature for children predominantly depended upon written symbols (verbal) in print reproductions (visual) within the classical literal *versus* figurative distinction of language (Reddy 1979), the relationship between language and reality came into question within the contemporary view of language (Lakoff and Johnson 1999). A few examples will elucidate the problematic stance:

- the print reproductions or illustrations which were seen as a supplementary design to the written component became a literal device and connected directly to a physical object in the external world;
- this literal device narrows the "connection" to the concept behind the form (Evans and Green 2006); and
- as a result, this literal "sort of an art-form appendix" creation was sometimes seen as unusual visual imagery or

even as fiction – utterances or illustrations that are not used in everyday conversations in a natural way.

Concrete evidence for such a problematic stance is unequalled in ancient religious texts. The *Elijah's ascension to heaven* text is but one example.

Traditionally, the interpretation of this text was in the literal *versus* figurative distinctive approach towards language. This means that certain kinds of linguistic expressions which may provide evidence that the structure of the first writer's conceptual systems is reflected in the patterns of language, were neglected. In this unconscious simulation process, the promising meaning pole of an utterance that may evoke schemas with a local alias has traditionally, in the translation of children's literature, been surpassed by acknowledging the conscious linguistic forms and constructions alone. Consequently, the illustrative appeal differs hugely from the intended meaning. Within the traditional approach, the outcome of the illustration was unusual visual imagery or fiction, as the simulation in certain Picture Bibles for children displays.

That the meaning is not predictable from the integrated meanings of the individual words, hardly comes to mind in traditional translations and illustrations of this *Elijah's ascension to heaven* text. Likewise, the context in which the utterance occurs as well as the language-specific systematic structure of thought was neglected. In determining meaning in a ±3000 year-old text with a different language structure and cultural setting, there's surely more to vision than meets the eye.

Evidently, we need a theoretical framework for interpretation and to establish the relevant "connection" of the illustration in the translated text to the "image" in the symbolic function of language.

Cognitive linguistics is methodologically an appropriate framework for this study, since it modifies conscious rational thought by elucidating that knowledge is constructed by a conceptual system, and utterances are understood by mentally simulating their content. Philosophically, this study assumes that the language system itself can be seen as a window that enables the direct investigation of knowledge representation and the process of meaning construction (Evans and Green 2006). The aim is, firstly, to signal the intention of an ancient religious text as perceived methodologically in traditional literal translations and matching illustrations for children; secondly, to give the reader an idea about how exactly impenetrable and constrained a culture-bound text can be if interpreted without acknowledging concepts; and thirdly, to challenge traditional translation processes of children's literature by the recognition of the cognitive unconsciousness.

How exactly impenetrable and constrained a culture-bound text such as *Elijah's ascension to heaven* can be if translators do not acknowledge the three (at least) mentioned notions of language, will be made clear within the process of meaning construction. For the sake of the argument, only one word (*chariot*) in the example text will be used as an illustration of the entire text.

The Process of Meaning Construction

The expression of thoughts and ideas as a crucial function of language became effective by the use of symbols. Symbols are forms and meanings (two binding parts that are conventionally associated as in Figure 1-1) with which the forms are usually paired and which may be spoken (as in the ['tʃær.i.ət]-sound), written (an orthographic representation [chariot]) or signed (as in bkr, i.e. a head of a man, an open palm and the floor plan of a tent[3]). The associated image of the chariot (the illustration in Figure 1-1) defines not a specific referential meaning in the world, but the idea of a chariot (ordinate categorisation). This conventional idea or semantic content associated with the symbol conveys meaning.

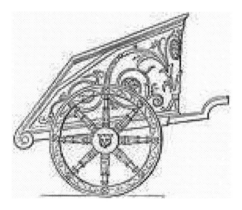

[bkr]/['tʃær.i.ət]

Fig. 1-1. Clipart ETC is copyright © 2003. Permission granted by the *Florida Centre for Instructional Technology* (FCIT), University of South Florida.

In the narrative of *Elijah's ascension to heaven*, the form/symbol *chariot* corresponds to a conventional meaning which is technically linked to a diverse range of perceptual information such as wheels, axles, reins, yoke, banner-staff, goading-stick, pole/wheels, pulled by a horse (or horses), armoured personnel carrier, vehicle and race and war chariot (Fretz 1982: 893-895). The form/symbol *chariot* thus "connects" to a mental representation termed *concept* rather than directly to a physical object in a particular context. Thus, the various perceptual information of *chariot* derived from the knowledge of the (mainly) ancient world is integrated into a single conscious *mental image*, which gives rise to the concept *chariot* (Evans and Green 2006: 6-7). A concept such as *chariot* is therefore a sensory perception that concerns perceptual data derived from a particular cultural context. From sensory experiences one knows that a chariot has physical attributes such as shape, weight, and colour, that a chariot occupies a particular circumscribed area of space.

Although the concept *chariot* can itself only be understood in terms of an object schema, an important finding in cognitive linguistics is that the conceptual system of the mind is expandable (Lakoff and Johnson 1999: 565). From literature akin to the cultural background of the Hebrew Bible, an important expansion for the concept *chariot* is cognisable. The object *chariot* as an open-class element (Evans and Green 2006: 193) elaborates as a culturally dependent function marker towards the following open-class semantic system:

- Some attributes such as "you ride in it" for the object *chariot* were functional attributes that seemed to require knowledge about humans, their activities, and the real world in order to be understood;
- Sun worship appears to have been associated with Solomon's temple and is associated in the book of Kings with the actions of Josiah, king of Judah (II Kings 23: 11). The erecting of model horses and chariots of the sun at the entrance to the sanctuary represented the conveyance in which the solar deity was believed to traverse the heavens. In Acadian hymns to *Shamash*, the deity is, indeed, described as "the chariot rider" (Stadelmann 1970: 73-74).
- The significance of the cloud theme as carriage in the Hebrew Bible can be seen in the expression "Yahweh, rider on cloud" (Isaiah 19: 1);
- The transformation or transmutation of language and "metaphorical thought" (not mythical thought) (Manjali 1997: 157-167) in II Kings 2: 1, 11 reflect a basic sensory experience transformed into the realm of "significance", the metaphoric-religious.

The same basic mental activity of simple sensory experience may be summarised as follows:

- *chariot*: (war) vehicle for human (warrior) to travel the earth;
- ♆: (war) vehicle for the sun (/deity warrior) to traverse the heaven (Deist 2000: 121).

A revelatory new connotative understanding is apparent which fulfils not a referential function anymore, but rather an expressive function in the text. The linguistic and metaphorical connotative thought encloses the entirety of the sense data, but only upon a "particular essence": From the functional attribute of *chariot* and the associated human activities, the capacity of the embodied mind to imitate others (Lakoff and Johnson 1999: 565) was employed. In the elaboration the human (warrior) was vividly imagined as being another (deity) warrior, doing what that deity does, experiencing what that deity experiences. "Experientially, this is a form of 'transcendence'. Through this, one can experience something akin to 'getting out of our bodies'–yet it is very much a bodily capacity" others (Lakoff and Johnson 1999: 565). Other than the "transcendence", spatially constrained regions were set up where movement exists in the bounded region of "here" versus in the separate space of "there". Thus, the "particular essence" of *chariot* resides in a primitive body-space relationship, bodily unity and spatiality that are inactively constituted, but also the transposition of the bodily unity and spatiality onto objects in space.

The new reference for *chariot* as "a (war) vehicle for the sun (/deity warrior) to traverse the heaven" is created. The new conception or idea is not separable from the actual, concrete and particular product but relevant to the creative writing insofar as it is connected with human life (Park 1982: 423). Theoretically, the new conception is the outline of a new way of being in the world, and a culturally emergent entity, token-of-a-type that exists embodied in physical objects (Margolis 1977: 45-50). Mentally, it is in the light of the projected world or worlds purpose that actual life can be better perceived, critically examined, and evaluated. Creative writing enriches our lives, because it allows us to live different lives we can never live in reality; it is inseparably related to our concrete and actual life, to our real world (Park 1982: 424). Thus, it appears that *chariot* in the culture-bound language is assumed to have a particular connotative/metaphorical meaning of its own, which may shed some light on the sender's intention. Pragmatically, this technique exists in different proportions in literary prose and is used in such a way as to draw the perceiver's conscious attention (Jackendoff and Aaron 1991: 333).

One way of dealing with such culture-bound connotative meaning in translation is to use the philological translation method (Nord 1997: 49) as employed frequently in the translation of ancient texts. According to this method, an explanation about the source culture or the regarded peculiarity of the use of *chariot* may be added as a footnote or glossary to the literal text.

However, a thorough assessment of utilising this method points to the following weaknesses which contravene recent findings in language acquisition and language understanding:

- unrealistic sentences describing incompatible visual imagery impedes decision tasks (Zwann 2002), while
- fictive motion sentences describing paths that require longer time, span a greater distance, or involve more obstacles, impede decision task (Matlock 2000).

For a translation to be a purposeful activity, the appellative function must reflect the shared experience or must work on account of cultural knowledge. This knowledge includes the cultural function of a text in its world of origin, as well as the cultural worlds discussed in or presupposed by such text (Deist 2000: 51). Therefore, one of the consequences for the concept of vertical translation in the functional approach to translation is that "functional units or components that are specific to the source culture "...have to be adapted in order to meet the requirements of the target situation" (Nord 1997: 70). This is possible if the rich conceptualisations of *chariot* are recognised by and accessible to the readers. If the process of transmission by the writer, and decoding and interpretation by the reader, which includes the process that involves the *construction* of rich conceptualisations fails, the interactive function of language also fails. A proper way for successful communication between the writer and the reader is what Schiffer in *Meaning* (1972) called "mutual knowledge". Mutual knowledge presupposes the clue established by the reader's knowledge of what the writer's words mean (symbolic function), as well as the reader's knowledge of the context in which the communication took place (interactive function). The clue left by the speaker/writer is nothing else than the tools, that is, the words and constructions, which the writer produces to evoke a particular understanding (Fillmore 1982: 112). This process of transmission, decoding and interpretation involves the construction of rich conceptualisations (Evans and Green 2006: 9).

The challenge, therefore, is to employ a similar embodied conceptualisation schema in the translation of this strangely regarded culture-bound text. The reason is twofold: firstly, an acknowledgment (from a linguistic point of view) the embodied experience of the "mirror" neurons (Gallese *et al.*

1996: 593-609) when "an action was carried out", for example, a warrior rides in the chariot, and when "the same/a similar action was seen", for example, the sun traversing the heaven; and secondly, an acknowledgment of (from a literary point of view) the frame of experience, indexing and even the construction of a particular context of *chariot* creates in the narrative.

Embodiment and Simulation

Cognitive linguistics holds that embodied experiences give rise to image schemas within the conceptual system (Johnson 1987). This means, as Kant in *Critique of Pure Reason* (1988 edn.) emphasised, that more abstract structures or schemas "lie at the foundation of our sensuous concepts" (Kant 1781/1988: 119). A striking consequence for language is that abstract thought has a bodily basis. Schemas are thus structures of imagination that connect sense perception with the concept of understanding, and therefore render significance to the phenomena. Image schemas as schematic representations are derived from the following embodied experiences:

- recurrent bodily activities of sense perception, movement and balance (vestibular system);
- perceptual modalities such as the tactile (haptic system);
- perceptual modalities such as the visual (visual system); and
- an auditory system where the sensory experience of hearing is located (Croft and Cruse 2004: 44).

Image schemas are thus imaginatively constituted, preconceptual structures upon which later conceptual processes and development take place. Because of the involvement of the body in the constitution of these schemas, they are also referred to as "embodied" schemas.

In translating a text such as *Elijah's ascension to heaven* and consequently illustrating the text for children, at least the sensuous experience of movement within the image schema of locomotion[4] of the culture-bounded symbol [chariot] must be taken into account. Thereafter the translator can exploit the option to change the expressive function of the symbol [chariot] to the referential function in order to meet the meaning in the text:

Sensuous experience of *Movement*

Movement: Walk – body (not fast, possibility of getting tired, can handle a weapon);
Movement: Run – body (faster than walk, but with the possibility of getting tired quicker; if tired, cannot easily handle a weapon);
Movement: On (*constraint*) a horse – bodily functions transferred to a stronger body (faster than run, possibility of "stronger body" getting tired, cannot handle weapon easily);
Movement: In (*constraint*) a chariot pulled by horses – double strong body (fast movement, no possibility of getting tired easily, can easily handle a weapon).

Language assists people in understanding new things in the light of the known. Accordingly, this sensuous experience of movement forms a mapping domain for the abstract entity – sun movement. In the Mesopotamian and Canaanite pantheon, the sun was experienced to traverse the heaven (as a warrior deity) (Deist 2000: 119-121).

What is important is that these schemas are structures which interpret and frame our experiences, expressions and comprehension before any logico-combinatory operation can take place upon the conceptual units (Manjali 1997: 159). This means that new experiences such as "the movement of the sun at day" are metaphorically understood and expressed in terms of the already available embodied schemas. In this way, the embodied schemas of concrete objects and situations are employed to make sense of more abstract entities and events.

An embodied approach towards culture-bound texts such as the *Elijah's ascension to heaven* testimonial within the background of traditional literal interpretations of religious texts, can do justice to the meaning of the text. Applying the embodied approach, the "unusual visual imagery" as discussed can fulfil its appellative function again in its linguistic register.

Conclusion

The relevance of embodied experiences as the heart of meaning
construction–opposed to traditional literal approaches and the resulting
simulation of unusual visual imagery–brings new perspectives for the
translation of children's literature into the open: Firstly, translation for
children is no longer a random "matching" of the verbal and the visual, but
it is a systematic dependence upon embodied concepts. Secondly, the
recognition of image schemas plays a pivotal role in a culture's
"illustration" of reality; and thirdly, from the cognitive linguistic approach,
it appears as if the relationship and the "meeting place" between linguistic
and literary language is also to be found within a conceptualised system.

Works Cited

Croft, W and Cruse, DA. *Cognitive Linguistics*. Cambridge: Cambridge University Press, 2004.

Deist, FE. *The Material Culture of the Bible. An Introduction*. Sheffield: Sheffield Academic Press, 2000.

Donald, M. "Art in Cognitive Evolution." In *The Artful Mind*, edited by Turner, M, 3-20. Oxford: Oxford University Press, 2006.

Evans, V and Green M. *Cognitive Linguistics. An Introduction*. London: Lawrence Erlbaum Associates, 2006.

Fillmore, CJ. "Scenes-and-frames semantics." *Linguistic Structures Processing*, (1977): 55-81. Amsterdam: North-Holland.

—. "Frame Semantics." *Linguistics in the Morning Calm*, The Linguistic Society of Korea, (1982): 111-137. Seoul: Hanshin.

Fretz, MJ. "Weapons and Implements of War." *Theological Dictionary of the Old Testament*, edited by Botterweck, GJ and Ringgren H, 893-895. Grand Rapids: Eerdmans, 1982.

Gallese, V, Fadiga, L, Fogassi, L and Rizzolatti, G. "Action Recognition in the Premotor Cortex." *Grain* 119 (1996): 593-609.

Jackendoff, R and Aaron D. Review Works: "More than Cool Reason: A Field Guide to Poetic Metaphor by George Lakoff and Mark Turner." *Language* 67/2 (1991): 320-338.

Johnson, M. *The Body in the Mind–the Bodily Basis of Meaning, Imagination and Reason*. Chicago: University of Chicago Press, 1987.

Kant, I. *Critique of Pure Reason*. Translated by JMD Meiklejohn. London: JM Dent and Sons, 1988 edition. (First German edition, 1781).

Lakoff G and Johnson, M. *Metaphors We Live By*. Chicago and London: The University of Chicago Press, 1980.

—. *Philosophy in the Flesh. The Embodied Mind and Its Challenge to Western Thought*. New York: Basic Books, 1999.

Manjali, FD. "On the Spatial Basis of Conceptual Metaphors." *International Journal of Communication* 7, 1-2 (1997): 157-167.

Margolis, J. "The Ontological Peculiarity of Works of Art." *The Journal of Aesthetics and Art Criticism*. 36/1 (1977): 45-50.

Matlock, T. *How Real is Fictive Motion*. Ph.D. Thesis. Santa Cruz, CA. University of California Santa Cruz, 2000.

Nord, C. *Translating as a Purposeful Activity. Functionalist Approaches Explained*. Manchester, U.K.: St. Jerome Publishers, 1997.

Park, Y. "The Function of Fiction." *Philosophy and Phenomenological Research*, 42/3 (1982): 416-424.

Putnam, H. *Representation and Reality*. Cambridge, MA: MIT Press,
1988.

Reddy, M. "The Conduit Metaphor." In *Metaphor and Though,* edited by
Ortony, A, 284-324. Cambridge: Cambridge University Press, 1979.

Rohrer, TC. "Embodiment and Experientialism." In *The Oxford Handbook
of Cognitive Linguistics* edited by Geeraerts, D and Cuyckens H.
Oxford: Oxford University Press, 2007.

Schart, A. "Die Ordnung des Hebräischen Alphabets." *Kleine Arbeiten
zum Alten und Neuen Testament,* 4/5 (2003): 239-255. Waltrop:
Spenner.

Schiffer, S. *Meaning*. Oxford: Clarendon, 1972.

Stadelmann, LIJ. *The Hebrew Conception of the World*. Rome: Biblical
Institute Press, 1970.

Zwaan, RA, Stafield, RA and Yaxley, RH. "Do Language Comprehenders
Routinely Represent the Shapes of Objects?" In *Psychological Science*,
13 (2002): 168-171.

Notes

[1] II Kings 2:1, 11 in the Hebrew Bible.

[2] The definition that I will use of *embodiment* here is "the claim that human physical,
cognitive, and social embodiment ground our conceptual and linguistic systems"
(Rohrer 2007: 5).

[3] Bodily and culturally-based script pictures from Proto-Sinaitic (see also Schart,
Die Ordnung des Hebräischen Alphabets, 253-254).

[4] See Evans and Green, *Cognitive Linguistics*, 190 for a list of image schemas.

PART II:

TRANSLATION CHALLENGES

CHAPTER THREE

"CONTENT FOLLOWS CONTEXT"[1]: TRANSLATING THE BIBLE FOR CHILDREN[2]

JAQUELINE S. DU TOIT, UNIVERSITY OF THE FREE STATE, SOUTH AFRICA

Introduction

Children's bibles published for lap readers (Retief 1990: 36) are colourful representations of dour (traditionally clad in black/white leather) adult translations of ancient Hebrew and Greek source texts. This contrasting sensory description is indicative of the disjunctive knowledge transfer between the black-and-white revered, standardized, "adult" translation, and the informal, almost irreverent childhood renderings. Nevertheless, children's bibles are still presumed divinely inspired in Judaeo-Christian tradition, if not directly derived from God.

Therefore, though scholarship may assume a critical approach to the source text(s) and their origins, the pre-critical assumptions of religious traditions still holds true for children's bibles. The non-critical assumption of source text inviolability was first enforced by emergent Protestantism (Bottigheimer 1996: 14-37, Gold 2004: 78, 191). Yet, despite the sacredness in which adult and juvenile version was hereby cloaked, many canonical taboos were broken in children's bible translation: title insertion, the exclusion and sanitizing of troubling texts, simplification, pictures, and the disruption of canonical sequence all pose problems for the notion of a divinely inspired, letter-perfect, "accurate" and "faithful" translation. Of these, the selection principle proves most difficult to account for: both of particular story sections and preference for one "adult" translation over another as intermediary source for purposes of translation. Hardly any children's bible translation makes use of the original source texts, but few would indicate their source as anything but. Because the tradition holds that the source texts were divinely inspired, rendering them (and by extension, their authoritative translations), canonical and governed by the principle of a letter perfect text (cf. Levy 2001: 4) with the accompanying dictum of divine retribution against alteration. This did not inhibit the translation of the bible since antiquity, but carried with it the *presumption* of literal conveyance of meaning by means of authoritative translation.

Authority nonetheless came to rest more on some translations such as the *King James Version* for the English speaking world. In fact, "Christians typically try out an unfamiliar translation for up to five years, using it alongside one they know and trust, before making the new translation their principal Bible" (Dewey 2004: 24). Much of the resistance to change relies on "faithfulness" imparted on some translations by the religious collectivity: "Faithfulness to the text and message of the Bible is a matter of great importance … [It] is a matter of top priority for us in the field of translation. … I think it is true to say that in many places our constituencies see the Bible Society in the role of custodian of the pure text of the Bible" (Fry 1999: 7). Thus, faithfulness, the preservation of "purity" in translation, or the *claim* thereto, is vital to bible translation for the tradition.

In South Africa, the presence of any number of intermediary "source texts" have to be accounted for in children's bibles, as most are translated from source texts originating in the United States or Great Britain. This is part of the general trend towards "internationalism" (Bottigheimer 1996: 48) in the twentieth century development of supra-confessional publications. For South Africa, little data exists for the status of these publications in the industry and a significant part of the publication/translation activity occurs outside the sphere of traditional publishing houses, in the realms of church and synagogue. Often, as for the rising evangelical churches, the resultant publications are directly linked to American versions of the same. Hence, many of the following observations on children's bibles in South Africa, are universally applicable to translations all over the world.

The categorization dilemma

The quandary of what children's bibles represent in the spectrum of a juvenile literary corpus is confirmed by the summary dismissal of children's bibles as neither "bible" nor "children's literature" in scholarly discourse (Du Toit 1995: 295, Demers 1993: 5). This resulted in a dearth in scholarship, accompanied by discomfort in how to account for the co-dependence of text and picture in the face of professed Judaeo-Christian aniconism.

Such negation of categorization may partly stem from the need to preserve prescriptive control over the presentation of translation and interpretation of a religious corpus. But this becomes difficult when the normative presentation for the book religion - words on paper - is adapted for the inclusion of alternative mediums of knowledge transfer, such as pictures, as Fry (1999: 8) explains:

> When [translators] move away from the medium of print, however, I think we soon find that our present concept of faithfulness is no longer fully adequate to cover or control what goes on in the presentation of the biblical text. This is because we have to move beyond the area of equivalence at the word, sentence, and paragraph level (although this still remains as a consideration), out into the area of wider discourse and communication factors which relate to the presentation of the message as a whole. In many cases we can no longer easily identify a presentation of the text as the 'closest equivalent' of a unit of the source text.

Yet, although religious tradition may contribute to the fear of translational loss of "control", all children's picture books suffer the same phenomenological difficulties because,

> Picture books ... break boundaries ... Disregarding literary norms, picture books often go to the extreme and the excess and include fragmentation, decanonization, irony, and hybridization ... What picture books have in common is their versatility and the various relationships of the verbal and the visual. Sometimes it is the visual that takes on and tells the story; sometimes the verbal takes over. And it is always the reader of the picture book that fills in the gaps and creates a new story ... (Oittinen 2003: 130).

Thus, secular and religious children's translation show broad similarities. And, despite the negation of children's bibles as a category of the former, they both conform to Shavit's (2006: 25) description of such literature as including "traditionally discussed translated texts", but also "abridgements and adaptations."

Children's bibles and orality: the parental/custodial intermediary

Shavit (2006: 25) mentions that the translation process, for children, takes place on two levels: "translations of texts from one language to another, but also the translations of texts from one system to another – for example, translations from the adult system into the children's." For religious literature it is more complex: as for secular picture books, an adult intermediary is required to read/interpret/translate text and image to the child audience, enhancing the experience by including their own interpretation/translation in the performance thereof (Oittinen 2006: 93). But for religious texts, this intermediary is not an adjunct, but a necessity to assist in the transfer of difficult moral/ethical material, as the primary function of the stories are didactic and not entertainment. Gold (2004: ix) describes the role assigned the parent/custodian as something she inherited from her Jewish religious tradition: "the right thing to do". She relays a common, but disturbing anecdote to illustrate how this "cherished ritual" of "quiet, intimate communication of love and truth"–reading aloud, followed by interactive participation in the hermeneutics of picture and text (provided by the parent from tradition, but prompted by the pictures)– works:

> Reading stories at bedtime was a cherished ritual throughout my child's early years ... sitting on the bed, one of my arms around Jeremy and the other on the book, we ended together a busy, active day.
> When my son was four, I thought it time to include some Bible stories. It seemed the right thing to do for a Jewish child. The first one I picked was a telling of the story of Noah's ark by Peter Speier, an award-winning book found on many lists of recommended books for children. I told the story many times, prompted by the detailed pictures in Speier's wordless book. Then one evening Jeremy stopped me at one picture, which showed crowds of animals gathered at the ark, water lapping at their knees, and only two of each animal walking up the ramp of the ark. "What happened to all the other animals?" my son asked. His question pulled into the foreground disturbing moral implications that my retelling of the story had ignored.
> "They died," I said. "Why?" he asked. I had no answer. I never read this book to my son again.

The pre-eminence of the adult mediator as translator and interpreter vis-à-vis the text/picture, mimics the orality of the Hebrew source where the narrator of the oral narrative had a prominent role in enactment, adaptation and interpretation. Hence, Dollerup's argument (2003: 83) for a separate development for texts meant to be read aloud, bears out: "... children's literature meant for reading aloud has a (pre)history different from that of children's literature meant for ... reading on your own." Dollerup argues for a body of literature *intended* to be read aloud to children, as opposed to a corpus for silent reading. This distinction is important here, as the presence of an adult narrator is necessitated, but also because orality is such an important underpinning thereof. Thus a children's bible has to recall both the oral tradition underlying the source text and the oral transfer of the target text.

Furniss (2004) emphasizes why the oral communicative moment is of such interest: it is in understanding its dynamics that the how and the why of the transmission of ideas and values, information and identities can be understood and the differing cultural parameters within which the process operates from context to context and from society to society can be observed. The flexibility of the orally transferred target text is therefore entirely dependent on contextualization to the didactic requirements of a very specific societal context. This fits a description of children's bible translation despite a religious tradition that purports to function according to the very opposite norm of constancy. The question is: how do children's bibles tolerate this inconsistency?

"Translated but improved"

Children's bibles are pseudepigraphal: that is, God is in most instances indicated as the direct or indirect author of the text in lieu of the human author and translator. And so, legitimacy in the tradition is established by means of this assertion of divine authorship. Thus, very few children's bibles prominently indicate, if at all, the name of the translator: the translation supposes divine inspiration and assigns to the translated text divine authority with little recognition of a translator's intervention. Legitimacy is thus imparted on the translations despite vast adaptation from source to target text. The presumption is that the children's bible is a "true", "accurate" and "faithful", albeit simplified, rendition of the original source and within the parameters of the canon. Hence these translations often presume (but rarely imply) a literal, functionally equivalent rendering of the original source text. Although evidently not the case for the often highly condensed and simplified lap reader versions, the *assumption* of literal translation without change or loss of meaning is made. Although cloaked in religious prohibition, this does not differ much from other children's translations:

> … all these translational procedures are permitted only if conditioned by the translator's adherence to the following two principles on which translation of children is based: an adjustment of the text to make it appropriate and useful to the child, in accordance with what society regards (at a certain point in time) as educationally 'good for the child'; and an adjustment of plot, characterization, and language to prevailing society's perceptions of the child's ability to read and comprehend (Shavit 2006: 26).

The same unassailable moral and instructive agency, conveyed in didactic format, is inherent to the translation of children's bibles. This agency, often taken for granted given the religious nature of the content, is paramount in the assignment of medium and meaning.

The "Habit of Accuracy"[3]

> Those Protestants, Jews, and Muslims, … who express disdain for visual imagery in religious practice and seek to proscribe its use as "idolatrous" typically put in its place alternative forms of material culture that provide a different form of iconicity. … In each case, the text is a material expression of revealed truth that requires reverence as a physical presence of the holy, inasmuch as inappropriate treatment of the text is nothing less than disrespect for its author (Morgan 2005: 117).

For religion, despite claims otherwise, visual language is inextricable from the verbal. The text may have triumphed over the image in the profession of aniconicism, but in reality the iconic qualities were transferred to the text itself. Ironically, this "purging of images" escaped children's bibles. Illustrations have accompanied bible stories from the first (Bottigheimer 1996: 56). In fact, Bottigheimer (1996: 39) suggests that it may be the very move to aniconicity with the rise of Protestantism that may have brought bibles into the realm of children. Pictorial representation should therefore be considered essential to knowledge transfer in children's bibles and integral to the translation thereof as the religious tradition depends on the "sacred gaze" (Morgan 2005: 3) for the inculcation of the religious.

This is divergent from Goethals' description (1999: 163) of an "incorporation" of "visual representations in biblical translation." Here, the visual element is not additional to, but *inherently part of*, the translation and includes canonical meaning assigned to space and time, to colour, form and texture both in visual and verbal language and the all-important, often underestimated, interchange between the two.[4]

Lap readers follow the auditory cues provided by the adult mediator and "read" the accompanying pictures. The pictures are most often the only aspect read without the intervention of the intermediary by the target readership (cf. Lathey 2006: 4-5). Nevertheless, it represents the most neglected area of translation: most translators and publishers seem to believe that, although text may need translation and adaptation for new target audiences, no accompanying need exists for the visuals, assuming that images are untranslatable and/or universal. This may be because the illustrations are most often derivative of the title assigned the story, and titles are additions to the source text. As titles are therefore presumed to perform a summative function, the accompanying illustration presumably should do the same without need for alteration (cf. Gold 2004: 106), as the moral object lesson purports to be universal in the tradition.

It should therefore come as no surprise that very little or few instances of indigenization of images of Jesus, and other religious figures were found for the South African multi-cultural audience, except figures traditionally considered to have been people of colour, such as the Ethiopian of Acts (8: 26-40) (cf. e.g. Jander 2005a & 2005b). This is easily explained, as most source texts used for children's bible translation derive from the United States, and, as Bottigheimer (1996: 47) pointed out, "no children's Bibles have been composed specifically for African-American children in the United States, despite the existence of a long European and American tradition of identifying numerous biblical [figures] ... as African."

South African context

Bottigheimer's 1996 study of the historical development of children's bibles has clearly indicated that, despite pretensions to consistency and adherence to canon, the rendering of the bible to children has indeed shown remarkable adaptation to "reigning social assumptions" and the "reordering" of story content (1996: 217).

For a South African scholar in a linguistically (eleven official languages) and culturally diverse country where Christianity nevertheless predominates (79%), this raised an important question: to what extent would Bottigheimer's dictum of content following context hold for the unique environment in which mother tongue speakers of South African languages grow up? What would be the interchange between the translation of picture and text to account for this in the religious discourse? Sadly, I found a distressingly non-representative mono-culture represented by a predominance of English, with some Afrikaans translations, of children's bibles derived primarily from the US. This non-alignment of societal context and the contemporary South African children's bible made sense only once a questionnaire to representatives from various publishers, revealed that the publishing industry gives little cognisance to niche interests. Hence the target audience for children's literature is undifferentiated from the profile of the average South African reader described by the respondents as (Cawood 2005):

- Older (30 years plus);
- Well educated, but at least a high school certificate (matriculation);
- Access to literature at home, in shops and libraries;
- English/Afrikaans speaking;
- White; and
- Female.

This, combined with the continued movement towards internationalisation in the publishing industry, as evidenced by children's bible translations in South Africa, leads to a distressingly non-representative presentation of context in children's bibles in individual speech communities. Choice in representation, choice in narrative and choice in medium appropriate to the didactic requirements of the individual religious community, seems to be governed by the unifying factor of publication cost and may result in even greater homogenization in future. Thus it may follow that certain selections and representations of children's bible stories will become normative, rather than representative of societies' contextual demands, with inevitable exclusion, alienation and lack of individual identification with story content as the result.

Sadly, just as the right to choose arises as a real consideration in adult translation of the bible, this may be disappearing for children's bible translations. Euan Fry (1999: 12) refers to "choice" as "a very important question of principle" that becomes paramount once selection takes place to suit translation into different media.

In the past, evaluative adaptation, as defined by Shavit (2006: 38), allowed the translator of children's literature the freedom to, "completely change the source text in order to have the revised version serve ideological purposes," as the primary function of the transfer of knowledge was considered didactic. This not only involved an increased vocabulary and more complex sentence structures, but also the improved ability to adapt language and visual representation to the demands of the modern religious context. Nonetheless, the importance of alignment of translation strategies in visual and textual language was not often underscored. Partly because a source text selected, adapted and translated by adults and mediated by adult narrators, often left the only piece of text directly confronted by the child reader, the picture, unaccounted for in the translation. Greater cognisance therefore is needed of the fact that, as Gold (2004: 107) explains for Jewish children's bibles, that apart from language simplification,

... the writers also needed to alter the laconic and ambiguous narrative style of the biblical text, so they actually *added* material to the stories, elaborating on motivation and moral to insure that the audience would receive the appropriate ethical message.

This "appropriate ethical message", had to be enforced, rather than detracted from, in the accompanying visuals, as they often "translated" the assigned didactically imbued title, rather than the accompanying text. Visual language represents a matter in need of urgent attention in the translation of children's bibles, as for all children's literature, but falls by the wayside in the move towards internationalisation. The alignment and choice of appropriateness of message in both the textual and visual language cannot be underestimated given the contextual priorities assigned to children's bibles by Judaeo-Christian religion. This confirms the notion that children's bible translation are more similar than different from children's literature in general as Fernández (2006: 52) substantiates by what she refers to as "extra-textual factors".

Conclusion

This essay confirms that children's bibles are indeed part of the corpus of children's literature and as such, the concerns expressed regarding the homogenization of context for translated children's bibles, should indicate a grave concern for translators of secular children's literature as well. As the South African case study illustrates, Bottigheimer's dictum of content following context, ultimately a descriptive stance, no longer holds true for the translation of children's bibles. Financial concerns and the globalisation of the publishing industry, linked with the trend to follow the anglicized/Americanized(?) mono-culture of the marketplace, seems to prescribe rather than describe, the homogenization of selective source text translation and visual language for a homogenous, global target audience of children, irrespective of cultural diversification. This results in the creation of artificial rigidity in the translated text, ill describing the target audience, and the accompanying loss of the inherent flexibility of an underlying orality inherent to negotiation of knowledge transfer via a parental/custodial intermediary, integral to the convention of "reading" to lap readers.

Works Cited

Bottigheimer, Ruth. *The Bible for Children: From the Age of Gutenberg to the Present*. New Haven: Yale University, 1996.

Cawood, Stephanie. *Interviews with Respondents on the Publication of Children's Bibles in Indigenous South African Languages: the Current State of Affairs*. Unpublished Research Report Commissioned by Jaqueline S. du Toit & Luna Beard. Bloemfontein: University of the Free State, 2005.

Demers, Patricia. *Heaven upon Earth: The Form of Moral and Religious Children's Literature, to 1850*. Knoxville: University of Tennessee, 1993.

Dewey, David. *A User's Guide to Bible Translations: Making the Most of Different Versions*. Downers Grove: InterVarsity Press, 2004.

Dixon, John W. "Images of Truth: Religion and the Art of Seeing." *Ventures in Religion 3*. Atlanta: Scholars Press, 1996.

Dollerup, Cay. "Translation for reading aloud." *Meta* 48/1-2 (2003): 81-103.

Dowley, Tim. *Changing Picture Bible Stories*. Illustrated by Stuart Martin. Wellington: Lux Verbi. BM., 2006a.

—. *Kyk, die Prentjies Verander! Bybelverhale*. Illustrated by Stuart Martin. Wellington: Lux Verbi. BM., 2006b.

Du Toit, Jaqueline S. & Luna Beard. "The Publication of Children's Bibles in Indigenous South African Languages: an Investigation into the Current State of Affairs". *Journal for Semitics* 16/2 (2007): 297-311.

Du Toit, J. Wilna. *Resente Kleuter- en Kinderbybels in Afrikaans en Engels: 'n Krities-Evaluerende Ondersoek Binne 'n Literêr-Semantiese Raamwerk*. Ph.D. dissertation. Cape Town: University of Cape Town, 1995.

Fernández López, Marisa. "Translation Studies in Contemporary Children's Literature: A Comparison of Intercultural Ideological Factors." In *The Translation of Children's Literature: A Reader*, edited by Gillian Lathey. Topics in Translation 31. Clevedon: Multilingual Matters Ltd, (2006): 41-53.

Fry, Euan McG. "Faithfulness–a Wider Perspective." In *Fidelity and Translation: Communicating the Bible in New Media*, edited by Paul A. Soukup & Robert Hodgson. Franklin, Wis.: Sheed & Ward, 1999: 7-27.

Furniss, Graham. *Orality: The Power of the Spoken Word*. New York: Palgrave MacMillan, 2004.

Goethals, Gregor T.. "The Imaged Word: Aesthetics, Fidelity, and New Media Translations." In *Fidelity and Translation: Communicating the Bible in New Media,* edited by P. A. Soukup & R. Hodgson. Franklin, Wis.: Sheed & Ward, (1999): 133-172.

Gold, Penny Schine. *Making the Bible Modern: Children's Bibles and Jewish Education in Twentieth-Century America.* Ithaca: Cornell University, 2004.

Ham, Ken. *Dinosaurs of Eden: A Biblical Journey Through Time.* Illustrated by Earl & Bonita Snellenberger. Green Forest: Master Books, 2000.

Heilman, Samuel. *Defenders of the Faith: Inside Ultra-Orthodox Jewry.* New York: Schocken Books, 1992.

Jander, Martha Streufert. *Filippus en die Ethiopiër.* Translated by Morné van Rooyen. Illustrated by Kathey Mitter. Wellington: Lux Verbi. BM., 2005a.

—. *Philip and the Ethiopian.* Illustrated by Kathy Mitter. Wellington: Lux Verbi. BM., 2005b.

Lathey, Gillian. "Introduction." In *The Translation of Children's Literature: A Reader,* edited by Gillian Lathey. Topics in Translation 31. Clevedon: Multilingual Matters Ltd, (2006): 1-12.

Levy, B. Barry. *Fixing God's Torah: The Accuracy of the Hebrew Bible Text in Jewish Law.* Oxford: Oxford University Press, 2001.

Morgan, David. *The Sacred Gaze: Religious Visual Culture in Theory and Practice.* Berkeley: University of California, 2005.

Oittinen, Riitta. "Where the Wild Things Are: Translating Picture Books." *Meta* 48/1-2 (2003): 128-141.

—. "The Verbal and the Visual: On the Carnivalism and Dialogics of Translating for Children." In *The Translation of Children's Literature: A Reader,* edited by Gillian Lathey. Topics in Translation 31. Clevedon: Multilingual Matters Ltd, (2006): 84-97.

Retief, H. J. M. "Uitgee van kinderboeke." In *Kinder- en jeugboeke: referate gelewer tydens die HAUM-Daan Retief Simposium oor kinder- en jeugboeke,* edited by H. S. Coetzee & H. J. M. Retief. Pretoria: Universiteit van Pretoria, (1990): 84-97.

Shavit, Zohar. "Translation of Children's Literature." In *The Translation of Children's Literature: A Reader,* edited by Gillian Lathey. Topics in Translation 31. Clevedon: Multilingual Matters Ltd., (2006): 25-40.

Notes

[1] "More often than not, rewritings of Bible stories for child readers seem to proceed from clear social, if not political, intentions. (...) Content followed context" (Bottigheimer 1996: 71).

[2] This research is funded by the South African National Research Foundation. Any opinion, findings and conclusions or recommendations expressed in this material are those of the author and the NRF does not accept any liability in regard thereto.

[3] Dixon 1996: 198.

[4] Oittinen (2003: 130-131) identified three kinds of functional relationships between the verbal and visual in picture books: supportive (telling the same story through congruence); contradictory (the two versions stand in exact opposition); and simultaneous (that is, a side by side doubling of the story in words and pictures).

CHAPTER FOUR

VERBAL AND VISUAL TRANSLATIONS OF MIDDLE-EARTH: CULTURAL REFERENCES AND WORDPLAY IN *THE LORD OF THE RINGS*

MIQUEL PUJOL TUBAU, UNIVERSITY OF VIC

Introduction

In this paper I will deal with the translation strategies necessary to solve cultural references and wordplay issues in *The Lord of the Rings* as a case study of its translation into Catalan. These translation challenges have been analysed in charts. Together with this study on the verbal, this paper includes illustrated visual representations and the cinematographic adaptation of Tolkien's world by Peter Jackson.

These cultural references and wordplay are fundamental to understand the aim of the author, JRR Tolkien, of creating a mythology based on English culture. In that respect, in the translation process it should be established in advance which translation attitude (foreignisation or domestication) would best suit the end reader. Needless to say that this choice always depends on the final receiver of the text, but, in this specific project, I chose, whenever possible, a foreignizing option, because my intention is to enhance the elements that prove the author's will.

Besides, my aim is also to assess whether the verbal (translation into Catalan) and the visual (both the drawings and the film) manage to keep the author's aim.

The story is developed in a fantasy context. Therefore, I will start by providing some information on Tolkien's article *On fairy-stories*, which could be regarded as a guideline to his writings. I will then move to Middle-Earth, with some of the author's personal issues deemed interesting for this study. Finally, I will deal with problem-solving translation strategies accompanied by some examples of my study charts and the illustrations of such examples to assess whether the visual and verbal transposition has been achieved.

This analysis allows for an extrapolation to other books of fantasy, but the conclusions drawn should mainly be regarded as the result of a case study on the translation challenges of *The Lord of the Rings*.

On fairy-stories

In 1964, JRR Tolkien published the book *Tree and Leaf*, which includes the short story "Leaf by Niggle" and the essay "On fairy-stories", where he gives his opinion about all the topics that affect fairy-stories, a genre which the author raises to the highest standard.

At the very beginning, he speaks about his desire: "Fantasy, the making or glimpse of Other-worlds, was the heart of the desire of Faërie [the realm of fairy-tales]. I desired dragons with a profound desire." (Tolkien 1964: 40). This statement arises two desires of the author: on the one hand, dragons; and on the other, the making of a world in which such dragons could exist. These desires include escape from the "rawness and ugliness of modern European life" (1964: 56) into a world of wonder. In addition, another "primordial human desire" of Faërie is "to survey the depths of space and time" (1964: 18). Both are two of the main reasons behind Tolkien's creation of Middle-Earth. Tolkien argues that escape from the modern world is beneficial, and he defends its use with the following words:

> Why should a man be scorned if, finding himself in prison, he tries to get out and go home? Or if, when he cannot do so, he thinks he talks about other topics than jailers and prison-walls? The world outside has not become less real because the prisoner cannot see it. In using Escape in this way the critics have chosen the wrong word, and, what is more, they are confusing, not always by sincere error, the Escape of the Prisoner with the Flight of the Deserter. (1964: 54)

In his purpose for writing fantasy, he devises a three-stage process. It begins with Escape from the world we live in. It is followed by Recovery, the inevitable result of Escape. Tolkien coins the final step as Consolation, i.e the relief that the person feels at the end of the process. This Consolation derives from what Tolkien calls "eucatastrophe", the Happy Ending, a basic feature for a fairy-tale to be called so, as opposed to "dycatastrophe", the fate that the story seems to lead to before "eucatastrophe" suddenly takes place. Although stories may or may not have a Happy Ending, in Tolkien's structure for an ideal fairy-story both "dycatastrophe" and "eucatastrophe" are necessary for such Consolation to take place. In *The Lord of the Rings*, for instance, when after all the troubles Frodo finds himself in the Cracks of Doom, he decides not to fulfil his quest (dycatastrophe). To the reader's surprise, it is Gollum's action which finally completes the mission (eucatastrophe).

Tolkien believes that because of its unlikeness to the "real world", Fantasy is the most difficult Secondary World to be created in such a way that it has the inner consistency of reality. In his own words: "Anyone can say 'the green sun', but 'To make a Secondary World inside which the green sun will be credible... will probably require labour and thought, and will certainly demand a special skill" (1964: 45).

Shaping Middle-Earth, a world inside a mind

We will now shift to some biographical information on the author that justifies the statement that Tolkien created a believable mythology for his culture that could work as a real ancient past for England. This mythology develops in a Secondary World called Middle-Earth.

In his childhood, after his father's death, the family moved to Sarehole, near Birmingham, a place that made a deep impression on him and was to be the basis of the Shire and the Hobbits, one of his race creations. We can state that very episode as the birth of Middle-Earth in him.

In his early boyhood Tolkien's mother taught him, and fostered an innate love of philology and romance. He used to say, "I was born with a talent for language just as someone is born with a talent for music (...) As a child I was always inventing languages". Quoting his biographer, Carpenter (1967), he always maintained that his stories developed from this:

> The stories are made rather to provide a world for the language than the reverse. To me a name comes first and the history follows. But, of course, such a work as *The Lord of the Rings* has been edited as I thought would be stomached by readers. I now find that many would have liked much more. (Carpenter 1967: 36)

During the First World War, he served in Flanders. This period of his life proves fundamental for his mentally-formed world, for the aftermath of the war, a grey world covered in dust and destruction, instilled in him the need for a parallel world, out of that nightmare: this is where Middle-Earth comes from.

He wanted an alternative to having to teach Anglosaxon, however much he enjoyed that. He needed a free and romantic "alongside world", and he literally made one by his writing romance. Writing fantasy was therapeutic for Tolkien; it was his personal Escape.

The translation of a brand-new world; the translation of a culture

Taking all these hypothesis as true, and taking into account the many cultures and languages into which the book has been translated, we reckon it is important to consider the cultural and wordplay issues that appear during the translation process, even more so if we bear in mind the author's intention to create a British mythology using real elements. Tolkien was convinced that a great culture could only be so if it was accompanied by a great mythology. This fixed idea comes from his interest in the Scandinavian, Celtic, Latin and Greek cultures and their subsequent mythologies. Besides, in fantasy there always has to be a Primary World (our own) and a Secondary World where the action normally takes place. Tolkien's resource for linking them was the following paragraph, to be found in the Appendices of The Return of the King in a section called "On translation".

> In presenting the matter of the Red Book, as a history for people of today to read, the whole of the linguistic setting has been translated as far as possible into terms of our times. Only the languages alien to the Common Speech have been left in their original form; but these appear mainly in the names of persons and places. (Tolkien 1955: 1107)

Tolkien created a whole new world for the speakers of a self-made language that he coined Elvish, because every language, to be a language, needs speakers. Apart from the Elves, a traditional Celtic character that Tolkien redesigned, he inhabited his world with other races, nation-like characters with their own characteristics. Hobbits, Men and Ents[1] are three races that constantly appear in the corpus I collected. This fact is quite likely due to the interesting use the author makes of the language when creating their profile. This use involves a number of translation problems that obviously need a solution. In general, most of the terms in the corpus can be separated into cultural references, wordplay and coined words.

Studying cultural references and wordplay

As a previous step to the practical part of the study, for the sake of coherence and a holistic view, it is indispensable to make a stand for a translation direction. That is, paraphrasing Schleiermacher (in Venuti 1995: 100-103), to take a foreignizing or domesticating attitude towards the translation. Being quite wary of extremes, I have intentionally used both of them. Nonetheless, bearing in mind the intended Britishness of Middle-Earth and its people, and trying to draw the author and the source culture as near as possible to the target culture reader (as is the purpose of this project), I chose whenever needed, the foreignizing option. Such a choice would, maybe, lead the Catalan reader to feeling a strangeness towards the text, but I deem it is fundamental to maintain the Britishness of the source text. Thus, as many English cultural details as possible will be transferred into the text to be experienced by the Catalan reader.

This study includes a practical part: the translation and analysis of specific terms that imply a problem-solving process. These terms are analysed in charts, which include the term, its context in the book and the different possible solutions I put forward. The one that was eventually chosen after dismissing the other options appears in bold. Finally, the published translation in Catalan and Spanish were also included as parallel terms because, I reckon, a comparative linguistic study may be interesting to find appropriate solutions.

As has been already stated, Tolkien created Middle-Earth by using, among other means, British cultural references. Besides, one of the greatest creative interests of his work is the relationships he establishes between races, thus giving an example of how reality can be constructed inside an Other-world ("the inner consistency of reality"). Dwarves and elves, for instance, are long-time enemies, theoretically due to their past encounters.

On a different level, in the shaping of these links and profile of races, the race of Ents is to be particularly considered. They are very ancient creatures, half-men and half-trees. Due to their intended ancient origin, their language is very peculiar and colourful, and their vocabulary grows with the use of wordplay. The example that follows illustrates it:

Entmoot, p. 467	
Context	*"Where is **Entmoot**?" Pippin ventured to ask. "Hoo, eh? **Entmoot**?" said Treebeard, turning around. "It is not a place, it is a gathering of Ents.*
Solution	**Entrobada** (wordplay - wordplay) Entassemblea
Justification	I chose this option in order to maintain the coherence and "truthfulness" in the terms referring to the world of the Ents. At the same time, it is useful to keep the wordplay existing between activity and entity in the original language.
Catalan translation[2]	Assemblent
Spanish translation[3]	La Cámara de los Ents

If we take a glance at the visual translation of this term, we will realize that both in Ted Nasmith's drawing and in the film adaptation by Peter Jackson, the wordplay produced by the mistaking of activity and entity for Entmoot is well represented. Their visual representation is as follows:

Fig. 4-1. Copyright © Reproduced with permission of Ted Nasmith

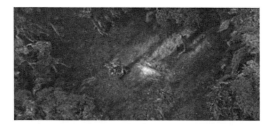

Fig. 4-2. Copyright © Reproduced with permission of New Line Cinema

We will now turn to cultural references as represented by the visual adaptations.

Their presence is very important in my corpus, especially as regards the races of Hobbits and Men. There are several inner cultures of Men in Tolkien's Middle-Earth, but the most interesting of them are the Riders of Rohan. To set their characteristics, Tolkien was clearly inspired by the Anglo-Saxon tradition. As a proof of it, I will provide an example of the corpus, the term "barrow":

barrow, p. 137	
Context	*Then suddenly he knew that he was imprisoned, caught hopelessly; he was in a barrow.*
Solution	**túmul**[4] (communicative translation)
Justification	It was a common practice amongst the ancient inhabitants of Britain (Anglo-Saxon and Celts) to bury their relatives in barrows. Such cultures did not exist in the ancient Catalan culture. However, pre-historical cultures in Catalonia used a similar funerary practice.
Catalan translation	túmul
Spanish translation	túmulo

In the following picture we observe a film representation of a "barrow" in the burial of King Théoden's son:

Fig. 4-3. Copyright © Reproduced with permission of New Line Cinema

The Riders of Rohan set a good example for another statement: visual translation can sum up many details in one single frame.

The following pictures depict two different moments of the story. In Anke-katrin Eiszmann's drawing, on the left, we appreciate the meeting of Aragorn, Gimli and Legolas with the outlaw Éomer and his faithful Éorlingas. In the film picture on the right we watch a detail of the Riders of Rohan just before they attack in the battle of Pelennor Fields. In both of them we appreciate the Anglo-Saxon characteristics of this race:

Fig. 4-4. Copyright ©   **Fig. 4-5.** Copyright © Reproduced with permission
Reproduced with permission of   of New Line Cinema.
Anke-Katrin Eiszmann.

Both the relationships between races and the unique language drive me to conclude that the book itself is a mixture of races, i.e. cultures. Therefore, I would state that in *The Lord of the Rings* we must consider the phenomenon of "metaculture" (a culture derived from another culture). Sometimes it does not technically create a problem, but it is worth taking it into consideration for the sake of cohesion and coherence in the text.

To solve the translation problems concerning cultural references I used the procedures developed by Hervey, Higgins and Haywood (1995), which are the following:

- Exoticism: keeping elements in the target text that enhance the foreign features of the source text.
- Cultural borrowing: Literal reproduction of the source text expression of which a corresponding cultural referent does not exist in the target culture. The context must help the reader understand the expression.
- Calque: Literal translation.
- Communicative translation: Substitution of the original expression by another in the target language as a communicative equivalence.
- Cultural transplantation: Substitution of the source context by a target context.

Before, I suggested that wordplay in *The Lord of the Rings* play a part in the story as a "metacultural" element. Therefore, I will explain the problem-solving procedures I chose for the analyses and translation of the wordplay included in my corpus. It is a compilation made by Dirk Delabastita of methods and techniques used in professional wordplay translation:

- Translating the ST wordplay with another wordplay in the TT
- Not managing to maintain a wordplay in the TT
- Using other rhetorical means
- Deleting the text fragment where the wordplay appears in the ST
- Reproducing the ST wordplay in its original form
- Compensating a previous loss by creating a new wordplay in the TT
- Adding new textual material containing a wordplay as a compensation for a previous loss
- Using editing techniques: footnotes, the translator's commentary in the prologue, etc.

I extended this list with a new category: the *portmanteau*, given that this creative technique is also found in this book. The term was coined by

Lewis Carroll and consists in a word formed by combining two other words. One example of my corpus could be as follows:

tweens, p. 21	
Context	*At that time Frodo was still in his **tweens**, as the hobbits called the irresponsible twenties between childhood and coming of age at thirty-three.*
Solution	era un adultescent **era un novintcell** (*portmanteau*)
Justification	In order to keep the *portmanteau*, I combined the separate translation of the words included in it: "*vint*" (twenty) and "*novell*" (apprentice), and so I could maintain the meaning Tolkien gives the "irresponsible twenties".
Catalan translation	Vintens
Spanish translation	En la "veintena"

This example is useful to prove that Tolkien used puns as a linguistic technique to create Middle-Earth. The solution suggested for this example demonstrates that some linguistic challenges have a possible verbal translation. On the contrary, the new reality that this term creates has no possible visual translation in illustrations or in the film adaptation. Therefore, one can assume that sometimes words describe elements that cannot be transferred in a visual translation.

Conclusions

As a conclusion to this paper, I would like to suggest that, as implied in by biographical data on the author, his own essays on fantasy and fairy-tales and specific vocabulary from the *The Lord of the Rings,* it could be claimed that Tolkien created a Secondary World, Middle-Earth, that holds enough characteristics to be a possible mythological world for the English culture, which would have certainly been different if Tolkien's cultural identity had been a different one.

Besides, the inner cultural issues in this would-be world must be considered. It stands as a unique example of intratextual culture in literature. All of these issues must be taken into account when analysing the translation in the fields we have, i.e. cultural references and wordplay.

As regards the translation process, I tried to maintain a coherence following the author's will of establishing cultural frames for his races, thus providing them with an identity that allowed his story to be inserted in a fantastic and also possible world.

Concerning the translation analysis and practice, I can assert that the method used proved to be very productive because, provided with a theoretical basis, it enhances reflection and coherence and develops the capacity to justify choices. This process allows the acquisition of translation routines based on motivated choices, which have been demonstrated to be highly important for the translator's work.

Works Cited

Carpenter, Humphrey. *J.R.R. Tolkien. A Bibliography*. London: Unwin.

Carroll, L. *The Annotated Alice. Alice's Adventures in Wonderland and Through the Looking-Glass*. London: Penguin Books, 1970.

Delabastita, D. (ed.) *Wordplay and Translation*. Special edition of *The Translator*, 2: 2. Manchester: St. Jerome; Namur: Facultés Universitaires Notre-Dame de la Paix, 1996.

Hervey, S.; Higgins, I.; Haywood, L. *Thinking Spanish Translation. A Course in Translation Method: Spanish to English*. London: Routledge, 1995.

Jackson, Peter. *The Lord of the Rings. The Fellowship of the Ring*. New Line Cinema (DVD), 2002.

—. *The Lord of the Rings. The Two Towers*. New Line Cinema (DVD), 2003.

—. *The Lord of the Rings. The Return of the King*. New Line Cinema (DVD), 2004.

Norman, P. 'The Hobbit Man', *Sunday Times Magazine*, 15 January 1967.

Tolkien, J.R.R. *El senyor dels anells*. [Translated by Francesc Parcerisas; 1st edition, 4th reprinting]. Barcelona: Editorial Vicens-Vives, 1986.

—. *El señor de los anillos*. [Translated by Luis Domenech, Matilde Hornos and Rubén Masera; 1st edition, 12th reprinting]. Barcelona: Ediciones Minotauro, 1995.

—. *The Lord of the Rings*. [Reedited from the Harper Collins 1966 Second edition]. London: Harper Collins Publishers, 1991.

—. *Tree and Leaf*. London: George Allen & Unwin Ltd., 1964.

Venuti, L. *The Translator's Invisibility: A History of Translation*. London: Routledge, 1995.

http://anke.edoras-art.de/ (online) [3rd December 2007]

http://www.tednasmith.com/ (online) [3rd December 2007]

Notes

[1] Capital letters are used when mentioning the races generically.

[2] The published Catalan translation was performed by Francesc Parcerisas.

[3] The published Spanish translation was performed by Luis Domènech, Matilde Horne and Rubén Masera.

[4] In the Catalan context, a "túmul" was a funerary element of pre-historic times having a similar shape to a barrow.

Chapter Five

Bearers of the Human Spirit: The Translator as a Social Activist

Salvador Simó, University of Vic

Translators are bearers of the human spirit.
—Alexander Pushkin

In this chapter I will reflect on the role of the translator in the contemporary world. I argue that the *scopos* and the situation, understood from an ecological and holistic perspective, determine this task. As translators, we must be aware of the ethical, social and political dimensions of our profession as bearers of the human spirit and to honour our responsibility towards present and future generations.

Translating for children

I share Riitta Oittinen's opinion (2000) when she affirms that situation and intention are intrinsic parts of all translation processes; we do not translate isolated words but complete situations. But, to outline our role, we must go further and develop an ecological vision, where ecology is "the relation, interaction, and dialogue between all existing things and with all that exists. Ecology is not just about nature but also about society and culture. Nothing exists outside this relationship. All is related with all in all the fragments" (Boff 2000: 19). This ecological attitude is called holism (from the Greek *holos*, meaning totality), a term coined by the philosopher Jan Smutts that describes "the effort to interpret the whole in the parts, and the parts in the whole" (Boff 2000: 23). We contribute to translation with our cultural heritage, our cosmovision, our image of childhood and our ideology. We enter into a dialectical relationship that includes the readers, the author, the illustrator, the publisher, the translator and their worlds.

This chapter proposes a translator-centred approach differing from approaches based on abstract concepts such as equivalence or fidelity. The intention or *scopos* and the situation, understood from an ecological and holistic perspective, are the two key points here; the ideal of equivalence is left behind as it presents an illusion of symmetry between the languages, which hardly exists beyond the level of vague approaches and which distorts the basic problems of the translation. The functionalist approach introduced by Reiss and Vermeer (1989) emphasises the importance of the *scopos*. Any form of translation is an action and all action has a purpose or intention. The word *scopos* denotes the technical concept of the purpose or intention of the translation. When we read, we write, we translate, or we illustrate, we are always in a situation to which we give a meaning. We must consider that all situations imply the translator having an ethical being and ideology. Translation is a deep and conscious process, involved in ethical, social and political dimensions. But we cannot forget the principle of loyalty. In the words of Nord (1991), loyalty is an indispensable moral principle in the relations between human beings, who are companions in the communication process.

When Nida discussed functional or dynamic equivalence, he concluded that the reactions of the readers of the translation have to be the same as those of the readers of the original text (cited in Gonzalez Davies 2004). But as Nord (1991/1999) points out: functional equivalence is not the normal *scopos* in translation, but an exceptional case in which the factor "change of functions" is assigned a zero value. A clear example is our story on the soldier children, *I did not want to do it*, whose original version in English is intended to facilitate therapy with soldier children in Sierra Leone, whereas its translation in Spanish is intended to create awareness among Spanish children of the reality of soldier children.

Story and ideology

John Stephens (1994: 8) in his book *Language and Ideology in Children's Fiction* affirms in relation to children's literature "what this otherwise rather amorphous body of text has in common is an impulse to intervene in the lives of children". Zipes (1983) affirms that the quality of a national culture depends on the socialisation developed by human beings to integrate young members in the society and to reinforce the norms and values which legitimise the sociopolitical system and which guarantee some sort of continuity in society. Language plays a fundamental role in understanding social life; it determines how the sense of self is constructed, and what mechanisms govern interpersonal relations and social hierarchies. Language, as a system of meaning, is endemically and pervasively imbued with ideology (Barthes 1972; Larrain 1979; Fairclough 1989).

This reflection is powerful and implies a great responsibility for those who want to write or to translate children's literature, because by doing so, instead of being agents of liberation, we can become accomplices in unfair sociopolitical systems based on the exploitation of the weakest. According to structuralist theory (Galheigo 2006), society is based on a consensus of all its parts. This ideal society must be maintained and protected from transgression. This theory sees the marginalized and excluded as problematic: they must re-adapt to re-enter society, as if one fine day they had decided to leave it. This theory is refuted, among others, by Marxist theory, according to which the origin of marginalisation is in the non-equitable distribution of wealth.

We can establish an analogy with feminist theories; carnivalism, whose purpose is to question the dominant ideological positions of the time; the critique of the Eurocentric approaches to fields that Haroldo and Augusto do Campos make in Brazil; or postcolonial theories, with the study of translation in relation to empire (Robinson 1997: 10), "the realization that translation has always been an indispensable channel of imperial conquest and occupation". Relations of power are at the basis of cultural studies. One contribution is the concept of translation norms suggested by the Polysystems theory which describes how translators operate within the restrictions imposed by the subjective idiosyncrasies that reflect the social and historical tendencies of the target community. The tendency is to adapt to norms, but a tension between central and peripheral texts exists, which reminds us of the dialectic between developed and developing countries. Power is the cause of social oppression.

The human being is a *bios politikos*, a carrier of ideology. One question prevails: what is our ideology as translators?

A translator for the contemporary world

Suffering, more than admiration, makes us think.
—Leonardo Boff 2000

To the different metaphors assigned to the translator, I believe that we can add the image of Rodin's *Le Penseur*. A reflective task prevails, as Mounier (mentioned by Esquirol 2001) teaches us: reflection preceeds action so that the reflection-action dialectic is a movement similar to that of the systole and diastole of the human heart. All translators must be very aware of their planetary citizenship (Boff 2000), and their social responsibility.

Context: a cultural and human genocide without precedent

We cannot only locate a text in its context. A translator does not exist in a vacuum. They are part of a historical process, a human epic, as the philosopher Gabriel Marcel would say. Our present context is marked by an acute crisis, to which I refer as genocide, in its cultural and human dimensions.

On the one hand, Wade Davis (2001) affirms that throughout human history around 10,000 languages have existed. Today, only 600 languages are considered safe. What is a language? For Davis it is a reflection of the human spirit, a complete ecosystem of ideas and institutions, a waterfall of thought, an age-old forest of the mind, the filter through which the soul of each particular culture is related to the world. It is an alive, divine and mysterious being. Most languages have yet to be recorded. In danger are spiritual, intellectual and artistic expression with all the complexity and the diversity of human experience.

On the other hand, according to the United Nations (2005), 20% of the population of the world lives in conditions of extreme poverty, without access to drinking water, education, health and food. The predictions are that if the present economic system continues this proportion will rise to 33% of humanity. Martin Monestier (1999) illustrates the situation of childhood. Children have become an integral part of the conflict. They are lost, separated from their families, abandoned, orphaned, tortured, mutilated, sexually abused, kidnapped, starved, forced to become soldiers, forced to kill. Some mines are specially designed to damage children and sexual abuse is particularly a threat for girls. UNICEF states that every day 40,000 children die because their basic needs are not met.

Ideology: an ethics for translation

What will become of translation studies? What gives sense to our existence? Towards which Íthaca shall we direct our ship? A paradigm is the shared common vision that professionals have of their own profession. As translators we must question what the ideology of our profession is. Are we simply a market-oriented profession or do we have a responsibility in the contemporary world? We cannot forget our ethical dimension.

According to Lévinas (1991), for whom ethics is the most fundamental kind of philosophy, everything is in the face. If we contemplate the face of that boy, of that girl, we will feel that values like freedom, equality, solidarity, justice, tolerance, peace must comprise our creed. What impact do we hope to exert on the children who read our translations? As Stephens states, "fiction must be seen as a special place for ideological influence, with a powerful potential capacity to model the attitude of the audience" (1994: 3).

Lecturers in translation faculties must ask themselves if they are educating citizens with an ethical commitment in their social reality, or mere technicians. I regard the figure of the translator as a cosmopolitan citizen, aware that humanity is our common destiny and that the Earth is our mother country (Boff 2000). For that reason, we must go beyond the education of translators and introduce in our university curricula Edgar Morin's reccomendations for the UNESCO (1999), the seven complex lessons in education for the future.

We must also consider our beliefs in relation to children. Elsewhere, I have defined the human being (Simó Algado 2004: 259) as "a physical, psychological and sociopolitical being, whose essence is spiritual and who is immersed in an ecological and cultural environment". The most controversial part of this definition is no doubt the human spirit. Spirit is a powerful, mysterious word; its meaning extends like a network through all levels of existence. It is air, breath, and, by extension, life and speech (Suzuki 2002). This reminds us of the affirmation that translators, when we bear language, bear the human spirit.

A contemporary translation

The translator can become a key figure to help provide an overall answer in the face of contemporary reality by giving priority to the translation of children's literature whose purpose is children's awareness of their planetary citizenship, and the translation of those texts which help to alleviate the situation of human or cultural genocide that we confront. That can be our way of co-operating to re-create the universe, through our knowledge, a way of fighting for beauty.

I will now analyse the criteria I would use to select translations of the verbal and the visual for a brief compilation of children's literature in the cited subject areas. In relation to culture and children's literature, Canada is an interesting example, with a special sensitivity in this field. Literature exists that reflects the culture of the First Nations, sometimes bilingual books, in English or French, and the native culture. Haida stories serve as examples, such as *Solomon's Tree* (Spalding and Wilson 2002), *Storm Boy*, (Lewis 1999); or Inuit stories like *Whale Snow* (Edwardson and Patterson 2004) or *Dreamstones* (Trottier and East 1999). For these stories, whose purpose is to preserve and to present indigenous culture, Venuti's (1986, 1995) foreignizing approach seems to be the most appropriate. We can choose this approach for *L'Afrique, petit Chaka* (*Africa, Small Chaka*, Sellier and Lesage 2003), which transmits African culture or *Buddha in the Garden* (Bouchard and Zhong-Yang Huang 2001), about Buddhist culture.

In relation to war there are stories like *De Keine soldaat*, (*The Small Soldier*, Verrept 2003), *Le petit garçon étoile* (*The Little Boy Star*, Hausfater-Douïeb and Latyk 2003); about refugees *El color de la arena*, (*The Colour of the Sand*, O'Callaghan and Santos 2005) or *The Colours of Home* (Lincoln 2002). If the purpose, *scopos*, of the translation is to present these realities to children, I would use the same foreignizing strategy, but if the purpose is therapeutic, to facilitate the emotional expression of the children, I would use a naturalization strategy, to increase the degree of identification of the reader with the protagonist of the story, thus increasing the power of the therapeutic metaphor: the stories serve as therapy because the children establish parallels between the story and their own life.

In *Über der Großen Fluss*, (*Beyond the Great River*, Beuscher and Hass 2004), and *No es fácil petit esquirol*, (*Small Squirrel, it is not Easy*, Ramon and Osuna 2003), the authors portray death through animal stories, in the first case a rabbit, a raccoon, a duck, an elephant and a mouse; in the second, squirrels. In order to increase the therapeutic potential, we could change the animal protagonists, in ecological contexts where these animals are not common. This strategy of naturalization could be repeated in *Peter's Place* (Grindley and Foreman 2003), which considers the environmental issues. It could be interesting to substitute the species that appear in the story with species present in the ecological niches of the readers, to help them to understand the value of what is lost when the environment is not cared for. Boys and girls can identify more with the necessity to preserve species that are known and loved, rather than distant strange species. If the purpose is more educational, for the reader to learn about other ecosystems, then a foreignising approach would be more suitable.

The translation of the visual

The visual and the verbal are the body and soul of children's literature. I believe the visual-verbal dialectic gives this genre its special beauty, turning the books into authentic works of art. In stories such as *Vi presento Klimt* (*I Present Klimt,* Capatti and Monaco 2004) the visual becomes more important. Modifying the images about child depression of *The Red Tree* created by Shaun Tan (2001), or the powerful illustrations about racism and intolerance of *Die Insel* (*The Island,* Saverländer and Verlag 2002) would change the message and effect drastically.

Fig. 5-1. The Red Tree, illustrated by Shaun Tan © 2005 Barbara Fiore Editora.

I consider that the same loyalty we demand for the verbal is necessary for the visual. Manipulation must be justified by important criteria, such as harnessing the therapeutic power of the story. It might be a good idea to change the ethnic origin of the protagonist or their sex, or the context of the story, to harness the therapeutic metaphor. In these cases I understand that the ideal is that manipulations of the visual be carried out by the original illustrator whenever this is possible.

For example, in *De Keine soldaat,* (*The Small Soldier,* Verrept 2003), the main character is a white boy, and the history is developed in a Western context. In a project for the therapeutic rehabilitation of former soldier children, with which I am collaborating with the NGO *Development and Education in Sierra Leone,* I would use a naturalization approach, transforming the verbal and the visual. The verbal will be modified to include African names, even the narrative could be expanded, reflecting more peculiarities of the experiences of the soldier children in Sierra Leone. The visual should be adapted too, in this case, reflecting the local ecological, cultural and social context.

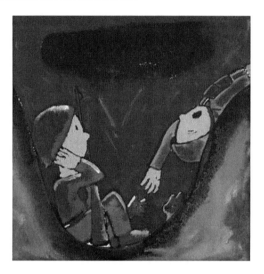

Fig. 5-2. *De Keine soldaat,* illustrated by P. Verrept [Translation: *El pequeño Soldado*] Copyright © Editorial Joventut. Reproduced by permission of Editorial Joventut.

Conclusion

We cannot go on being blind in the face of reality. This situation cannot leave us impassive. It is a call for social activism. We should remember in this conclusion the words of Federico Mayor Zaragoza (1999): "When we look at the future we find so many uncertainties about the world that our children will inherit. If we want this planet to satisfy the needs of its inhabitants, human society must transform". If we want the Earth to meet the needs of its inhabitants, human society must change. We are all responsible; we must fight to construct a sustainable and fair future. One of the greater challenges we face is how we can modify our way of thinking to meet the challenge of an ever more complex world. The old formulas no longer serve. The university cannot continue being an ivory tower, fragmented in knowledge fields, an intellectual bubble that turns away from contemporary reality. The indications of Edgar Morin can serve as a guide in this process. A small step, but a step, is the translation of books that can alleviate the suffering and pain that children are experiencing, to feed their spirit, to help to preserve cultural diversity, and to educate for cosmopolitan citizenship.

As Marcel (1995) said, hope means universal solidarity in progress towards the common ideal, to be faithful to this call until the aim is attained, against all odds. May this chapter serve, in all humility, to arouse the social activism of translators, to be counter-hegemonic, to reflect on the ethical and sociopolitical aspects of our work, on how we can and must contribute to present and coming generations, on how to bring about the vision of Alexander Pushkin and on how to turn us into bearers of the human spirit. As translators we should heed the call of Emily Dickinson (2000):

Hope is the thing with feathers
That perches in the soul,
And sings the tune--without the words,
And never stops at all.

Acknowledgement

To Maria González Davies and Richard Samson for their inestimable support.

Works Cited

Barthes, Roland. *Mythologies*. A Lavers (Trans). London: Cape, 1972.
Beuscher and Hass. *Über der Großen Fluss*. Spanish edition: *Más allá del gran río*. Translated by Christiane Reyes. Barcelona: Editorial Juventud, 2004.
Boff, Leonardo. *La dignidad de la tierra. Ecología, mundialización, espiritualidad. La emergencia de un nuevo paradigma*. Madrid: Editorial Trotta, 2000.
Bouchard, David and Huang, Zhong-Yang. *Buddha in the Garden*. Vancouver : Raincoast Books, 2001.
Capatti, Bérénice and Monaco, Octavia. *Vi presento Klimt*. Catalan edition: *Us presento a Klimt*. Translated by Mónica Torras Mingueza. Barcelona: Tuscania Editorial, 2004.
Davis, Wade. *Light at the Edge of the World*. Douglas & Mcintyre, 2001.
Dickinson, Emily. *The Complete Poems*. New York: Barleby. Com, 2000.

Edwardson, Dahl and Patterson, Annie. *Whale Snow*. Watertown, MA: Talewinds, A Charlesbridge Imprint, 2004.

Esquirol, Josep Maria. *Què és el personalisme. Introducció a la lectura d'Enmanuel Mounier*. Barcelona: Portic, 2001.

Fairclough, NL. *Language and Power*. London and New York: Longman, 1989.

Galheigo, Sandra. Terapia ocupacional en el campo social. In Kronenberg, Simó Algado and Pollard (eds). *Terapia ocupacional sin Fronteras: aprendiendo del espíritu de supervivientes*. Editorial Médica Panamericana, 2006.

Gonzalez Davies, Maria. *Multiple Voices in the Translation Classroom*. Amsterdam: John Benjamin Publishing, 2004.

Grindley, Sally and Foreman, Michael. *Peter's Place*. Spanish edition: *La Playa de Pedro*. Translated by Teresa Farran. Barcelona: Editorial Juventud, 2003.

Hausfater-Douïeb, Rachel and Latyk, Olivier. *Le petit garçon étoile*. Catalan edition: *El nen estel*. Translated by Elena Martín i Valls. Barcelona: Ediciones Baula, 2003.

Larrain, Jorge. *The Concept of Ideology*. London: Hutchinson, 1979.

Lévinas, Enmanuele. *Ética e Infinito*. Madrid: Visor, 1991.

Lewis, Paul. *Storm Boy*. Berkeley, CA: Tricycle Press, 1999.

Lincoln, Frances. *The Colours of Home*. Spanish edition: *Los colores de casa*. Translated by Fiona Marfà. Barcelona: Intermon Oxfam, 2002.

Marcel, Gabriel. *The Philosophy of Existentialism*. Translated by Manya Harari. New York: Carol Publishing Group, 1995.

Mayor Zaragoza, Federico. Preface of the UNESCO document *Seven Complex Lessons in Education for the Future*. Paris: UNESCO http/:unesdoc.unesco.org/images/0011/001177/117740so.pdf, 1999.

Monestier, Martín. *Los Niños Esclavos*. Madrid: Alianza Editorial, 1999.

Morin, Edgar. The Seven Complex Lessons in Education for Future. http://unesdoc.unesco.org/images/0011/001177/117740eo.pdf, 1999.

Nord, Christiane. *Text Analysis in Translation: Theory, Methodology and Didactic Application of a Model for Translation Oriented Text Analysis*. Translated by Nord and Penelope Sparrow. Amsterdam and Atlanta, Ga.: Rodopi, 1999.

O'Callaghan i Duch, Elena and Santos, Maria Jesús Heredero. *El color de la arena*. Zaragoza: Luís Vives, 2005.

Oittinen, Riittta. *Translating for Children*. London: Garland Publishing, Inc, 2000.

Ramón, Elisa and Osuna, Rosa. *No es fácil petit esquirol.* Spanish edition: *No es fácil pequeña ardilla.* Translated by Elisa Ramón. Pontevedra: editorial Kalandraka, 2003.

Robinson, Douglas. *Translation and empire. Postcolonial Theories Explained.* Manchester: St. Jerome Publishing, 1997.

Saverlandänder; Verlag. *Die Insel.* Spanish edition: *La isla.* Translated by Nuria Ventura. Salamanca: Lóguez Ediciones, 2002.

Sellier, Marie; Lesage, Marion. *L'Afrique petit Chaka.* Spanish edition: *África, pequeño Chaka.* Translated by P. Rozarena. Zaragoza: Editorial Luis Vives, 2003.

Simó i Algado, Salvador. Occupational Therapy Intervention with Children Survivors of War. In Kronenberg, Simó Algado, Pollard: *Occupational Therapy without Borders, Learning from the Spirit of Survivors.* Oxford: Churchill Livingstone, 2004.

Spalding, Andrea and Wilson, Janet. *Solomon's Tree.* BC: Orca Book Publishers, 2002.

Stephens, John. *Language and Ideology in Children's Fiction.* New York: Longman Publisher, 1994.

Suzuki, David. *The Sacred Balance.* Vancouver/Toronto: Grestone Books, 2002.

Tan, Shaun. *The Red Tree.* Thomas C. Lothian Pty Ltd, 2001.

Trottier, Maxine and East, Estella. *Dreamstones.* Toronto: Stoddart Kids, 1999.

United Nations (UN). *Human Development Report 2005—International Cooperation at a Crossroads: Aid, Trade and Security in an Unequal World.* http://hdr.undp.org/reports/global/2005/pdf/HDR05_chapter_1.pdf, 2005.

Venuti, Lawrence. The Translator's Invisibility. *Criticism* 28 (Spring):179-212, 1986.

—. *The Translator's Invisibility.* New York & London: Routledge, 1995.

Vermeer, Hans J. Skopos and comision in translational action. In Andrew Chesterman (ed) *Readings in Translation Theory,* 173-87. Loimaa: Finn Lectura, 1989.

Verrept, Paul. *The Kleine soldaat.* Spanish edition: *El pequeño soldado.* Translated by Élodie Bourgeois. Barcelona: Editorial Juventud, 2003.

Zipes, Jack. *Fairy Tales and the Art of Subversion.* London: Heinemann, 1983.

PART III:

CHILD IMAGES

CHAPTER SIX

WHEN *TANTE PATENT EN DE GROTE SOF* FOUND *UN VIKINGO EN EL JARDÍN* (*A VIKING IN THE GARDEN*)

NEUS ESPAÑOL CASTELLÀ

Introduction

Tante Patent en de grote Sof (Aunty Tiptop and the Big Flop, suggested translation for an English version) is a fiction novel full of fantasy and imagination addressed to readers of 9 years old and above. The stories of Tante Patent were first published in black and white as comic strips in May 1962, in various provincial Dutch daily newspapers. Annie M.G. Schmidt would write the texts and Fiep Westendorp would illustrate them. There were four different strips the first of which, *Tante Patent en de grote Sof,* was included in a collection of stories called *Het beest met de achternaam* (The Beast with the Surname), published by Arbeiderspers in 1968. The story was revised and published again in 1988, this time as a book, and with new and coloured illustrations by Fiep Westendorp. We will be dealing with the Spanish edition appeared in 1997, published by Ediciones SM (Barco de vapor), and the Dutch edition from 1988 published by Querido, which reproduces the original black and white comic strip. The fact that the text is under the strips makes the scenes more comical, as it enables the child to read and look right away at the powerful, delicious and funny illustrations. This is if you read the original Dutch book; unfortunately for the Spanish readers, from my point of view, the Spanish translation, or 'visual' cultural transplantation[1] (Hervey, Higgins and Haywood, 1995) of *Tante Patent en de grote Sof* is less powerful, less delicious and less funny. Published in Spain in 1997 by SM Ediciones, Anne M.G. Schmidt's book was translated from Dutch into Spanish as *Un vikingo en el jardín* by Marc Lepêtre, and illustrated by Teresa Novoa. I contacted SM Ediciones and had the chance to talk to

Teresa Novoa about her work and the limitations the publishing house imposed on her when she was assigned the job. The format of the book and the title given to the Spanish story are the first striking differences. In the pages that follow I will illustrate the differences between both texts, and answer why the publishing house opted for an adaptation understood as a modification of the original Dutch story format.

As for the story itself, it describes the adventures of the smart and well-mannered *Tante Patent* after she discovers in her garden a sort of vase that belongs to a clumsy naughty *grote Sof.*

This is the power of illustrations: It doesn't matter if they are black and white or coloured, what matters is the influence and impact they have on children, in this case Dutch and Spanish readers, and how they can shape the children's minds.

From "Tante Patent en de grote Sof" to "Un vikingo en el jardín", remixed as "A Viking in Aunt Patent's Garden"

As stated in the introduction, the first striking differences between *Tante Patent* and its Spanish version are the format and title. In general, we could argue that the format, hardcover or paperback, is not so important but in this case it definitely is. The indicated age of the target readers in both books is 9-12 years old. However, the format and the type of illustrations on the Dutch hardcover and inside the book make it more visually attractive for children, whereas the Spanish paperback cover is more like the usual format of a book for young adults, where we find more text than illustrations. In other words, this is a clear example of a visual cultural transplantion, not so much at a text level but as far as the transfer of child images is concerned.

The Spanish title is another different feature between both books: It makes the story sound more adventurous and mysterious, and, in this case, more attractive to youngsters.

I believe that any Spanish reader would find *Un vikingo en el jardín* (A Viking in the Garden) more appealing than *La tía Patente y el gran Sof* (Aunty Patent and the Big Sof). The Spanish title is a valid choice because it is definitely an adventurous story. Even though the Dutch title is not humorous itself, the cover illustrations show us that humour will play a very important role in the story. They also introduce the two main characters and give us a hint about what will happen in the book. I find that something is lost already before we begin to read and view the story because the illustration on the Spanish cover does not reflect that humour and does not reveal any clues; this will somehow condition the readers, giving them an incomplete idea of what to expect from the book. When we look at the Dutch cover we cannot help smiling, whereas the Spanish illustration causes an indifferent or scary reaction.

Fig. 6-1. Dutch cover. Copyright © Querido. Reproduced by permission of Querido's Uitgeverij

Fig. 6-2. Spanish cover. Copyright © Querido. Reproduced by permission of Querido's Uitgeverij

When I first started to consider the reasons that led Ediciones SM to edit the story in paperback cover and choose the format they chose, I thought it was for budget reasons and with the objective of reaching a wider reading audience. But then I contacted the Spanish illustrator Teresa Novoa and she told me that "although fortunately there are always exceptions, it actually has to do with schools. The publishing house Ediciones SM, the owner of *Tante Patent*'s rights in Spain, works for schools editing collections of graded level books to be read in class or at home by the students on their own". There are specific criteria to be followed: "Books with illustrations and in colour are for children up to 6 years old; and for older children, books contain more text and only a few illustrations, usually black and white". This is basically why the publishing house opted for a visual cultural transplantation rather than for a translation that kept the original format. In this case, the book belongs to the "Barco de vapor" orange series; there is also a white series for first readers, a blue series for 7 year olds and up, and a red series for 12 year olds and up. Belonging to the same orange series and following the same criteria are, for example, the adaptations of Georgia Byng's *The Ramsbottom Rumble*, Urí Orlev's *The Monster in the Darkness,* or Angela Nanetti's *My Grandfather was a Cherry Tree.*

I wonder if Fiep Westendorp knew that Annie M.G. Schmidt's story was being adapted into Spanish and whether she had the chance to see her *Tante Patent* dressed as a Spanish aunty and her *Sof* as a ferocious viking. At this point, I will introduce the work of Dutch illustrator Sophia Maria Westendorp.

Author-Illustrator Collaboration in the Source Text

Generally known as Fiep, Sophia Maria Westendorp was born in Zaltbommel (The Netherlands) in 1916. She studied at the Royal College of Arts and Crafts in Hertogen-bosch. After a series of assignments for the Zaltbommel Tourist Information Office, on 20 April 1946 the first illustration by Fiep appeared in *Het Parool.* The editors of this newspaper used to meet at Café Scheltema. Fiep also went to this café regularly and one evening she literally ran into Annie M.G. Schmidt, and from that evening in 1947 onwards they remained friends. As stated in her website, www.fiepwestendorp.nl, of her collaboration with Annie, Fiep said: 'I always loved working with Annie. There was nobody I clicked with as well as with her. I think it was mainly humour that united us, but there was something else as well: our insecurity. If I read out a text Annie had written, she would ask: "Do you really think it's funny too?" That was very important to Annie. Viceversa, I was glad if Annie looked at my drawings through those funny big glasses of hers and burst out laughing'. Fiep and Annie were always in very close touch about their work. In 1952 *Jip en Janeke* appeared on the children's page of *Het Parool,* the beginning of Fiep's collaboration with Annie M.G. Schmidt. She illustrated many stories by Schmidt and they created many characters together. In 1962 Fiep did the drawings for *Tante Patent,* and in 1988 she created new illustrations for this book, this time in colour. Her last project with Annie M.G. Schmidt was *Jorrie en Snorrie* in 1990. She died in February 2004, in Amsterdam (The Netherlands).

This account of Fiep's life and what she said about her collaboration with Annie M.G. Schmidt shows how important humour was for both Annie and Fiep. Apart from the fact that they became friends and they "clicked well", using Fiep's words, it is amazing how accurately the illustrator captured the words, the thoughts and the feelings of the writer and her characters in *Tante Patent*. As we will see, this does not happen in the Spanish version because the illustrations are not given the relevance they have, they even disappear. For instance, every single page on the Dutch text, from page 5 to page 104, is accompanied by a comic strip made up of three illustrations mostly (sometimes 2, sometimes 4). This means 99 illustrated pages. However, in the Spanish text we only have 8 illustrated pages: page 11 (The Batavian); page 29, (the Batavian "playing" with the vacuum cleaner); page 41 (the silhouettes of Tante Patent and the Batavian at night); page 53 (Mrs. Virus climbed on a tree and the Batavian); page 61 (Tante Patent, Augusto Beil and the Batavian on stage); page 69 (Dr. Virus, the Notary, Mr. Nop and the Batavian); page 81 (Mr. Nop); and page 87 (Mr. Doodle, an American tourist). Considering this significant difference in the number of illustrations in both works, it is difficult for the story to have the same humorous effect on its target readers. In relation to the number of illustrations, I asked the Spanish illustrator Teresa Novoa what she would do if she was assigned to do the illustrations of *Un vikingo en el jardín* again, and was given total freedom to do her job, and she said: "If I was to illustrate this story again today, I would include many more illustrations, without a doubt. And I would like to do it in a comic strip format; I think it is a perfect story to do so. Unfortunately, I don't think any Spanish publishing house would be interested in editing a book like this. A publishing house specialised in comics might, but then this kind of story is not the kind of story they would publish".

At this point, I would like to introduce Spanish illustrator Teresa Novoa. She was born in 1955, in Madrid (Spain), where she studied Architecture. She started to work in a publishing house when she was still at university, and later she worked in a school as an arts teacher. Eventually, she decided to become a full-time illustrator of children's books, and in 1997 she illustrated Marc Lepêtre's translation of *Un vikingo en el jardín*. In 1999 she won the prize "A la orilla del viento", for her illustrations of *El pájaro y la princesa* (The Bird and the Princess), and a year later she was selected for the exhibition "A todo color", organised by the Spanish Ministry of Culture. In April 2005, together with other graphic artists, she was selected to take part in the "Ilustrísimos" Exhibition which was an overview of children's and young adult's illustration in Spain, in the frame of the Bologna's Children's Book Fair, where Spain was the Guest of Honour. Also in 2005, but as a writer, she published *¿Cómo es el cocodrilo?* (What Does the Crocodile Look Like?), *¿De qué color es la cebra?* (What Colour Is the Zebra?), and *¿Quién sigue a un elefante?* (Who Is Following an Elephant?).

Her drawings for *Un vikingo en el jardín*, in black and white, and shades of grey (only the cover is coloured) illustrate specific moments in the story and only a few characters of the book are portrayed: The Batavian, Tante Patent, Mrs. Virus, Augusto Beil, Dr. Virus, Notary Nop and Mr. Doodle. Novoa plays skilfully with the black and white tonal range to represent day or night, and she does a fantastic job portraying the characters and creating the mysterious atmosphere that surrounds the story. Still, we miss something because the viking is more than scary and Aunty Patent is more than a coquettish woman. We understand that every illustrator sees things in a different way and has his or her own drawing style, but the emphasis is not on how characters are drawn here. It is what is missing about them by only looking at the Spanish illustrations. In the Spanish version the text is given more relevance than the illustrations, whereas in the Dutch story there is a balance. Fiep Westendorp's illustrations for *Tante Patent* interact skilfully with an already wonderful tale. Westendorp's drawings are so powerful that we know exactly what is going on in the story all the time and with all kind of details.

Fig. 6-3. Copyright © Querido. Reproduced by permission of
Querido's Uitgeverij

In relation to what I said above, Argentinean illustrator Gustavo Ariel Rosemffet, known as Gusti, says: "Every illustrator gives his or her own interpretation of a text, otherwise we would all draw the same. A good illustration is not only the one that is good aesthetically, but also the one that makes the good book more beautiful, better"; and about the collaboration between writer and illustrator he adds that "the writer of a text that is going to be illustrated is very aware of it, and while writing he or she leaves some room for the illustrator to fill in". This is what Fiep Westendorp did, but Teresa Novoa didn't have the opportunity to do so.

Although we already know the answer, I keep wondering why the Spanish publishing house could not take a halfway option using the original format as a comic strip, more fun and enjoyable for children. Teresa Novoa made it clear to me that it was not her decision whatsoever. The book was to be used for school purposes and even though this should not mean it should be boring or less fun, the criteria adopted by the publishing house led to limit the number of illustrated pages. Teresa Novoa explained to me that after she was assigned the job she was only told the name of the author, the number of illustrations to be done and that these should be in black and white. Further, the illustrator told me that this lack of information was completely normal in Spain a few years ago, and that there was barely any communication between illustrators and editors, or illustrators and writers, not even when they were Spanish. Now, 10 years after she did the illustrations for *Un vikingo en el jardín*, Teresa Novoa knows more about the original author and her work: "You will be surprised to know that thanks to your email I know more details about Annie M.G. Schmidt and that Fiep Westendorp was the illustrator. I checked on the Internet and I saw an illustration of Fiep Westendorp's Tante Patent and the viking. Fiep Westendorp was a fantastic illustrator. I am surprised that in the Netherlands the book was published in a comic format, it is a great idea!" And she added: "Fortunately, the communication we have nowadays with editors is much more fluid than back then; and Internet helps a lot". Nevertheless, 10 years ago, as Novoa put it, "Internet was not that accessible yet and it would have taken me several days to find information about Annie M.G. Schmidt. Moreover, in the conditions in which we sometimes work, always short on time, it would have been difficult to do it", so she only had the Spanish text as a guide to do the illustrations.

The characters: Do personalities change in translations?

Perhaps now we will understand why both versions differ so much, but let us focus on the characters and how they are portrayed. The two main characters are the "grote Sof", which becomes the "vikingo", "el bárbaro" or "el Señor Sof" in Spanish; and "Tante Patent", who becomes 'tía Patente'. Tante Patent is above all, as Annie M.G. Schmidt herself describes at the beginning of the story, a decent woman living in a decent house in a decent street. Looking at Fiep Westendorp's illustrations, we gather that she is an educated, elegant, smart, brave, naughty and adventurous woman, and also "with a strong character and full of energy" as Teresa Novoa gathered from the text.

Fig. 6- 4. Copyright © Querido.   **Fig. 6-5.** Copyright © Ediciones SM.
Reproduced by permission of   Reproduced by permission of Ediciones
Querido's Uitgeverij   SM

    When we look at Novoa's portraying of Tante Patent we do not see all that, we know more about her because we read the story. Details like Tante Patent's hat, the tulips in her garden, her smile, or her angry face are not present in the Spanish version where tía Patente only appears on page 61. I must say in favour of Teresa Novoa that it is very hard to work in the circumstances she did, with such a limited number of illustrations and so little information about the original text. It is easy to miss something and to find the main characters in the Spanish version lacking the expressiveness and intensity of the original characters.
    Sometimes differences in the rendering of a story or a character have an origin in the cultural vision or cultural tradition of a country; religious tradition plays also a fundamental role: for instance, Catalan illustrator and scriptwriter Roser Capdevila, known for her work *The Triplets*, said in an interview in the Spanish newspaper *La Vanguardia* that in Iran the bored witch that appears in her stories became a grandmother because Islam does not accept a witch as a character.
    In *Tante Patent en de grote Sof* and *Un vikingo en el jardín* we have

two cultural visions of an American tourist, two ways of dressing an American tourist according to the illustrator's cultural and personal background:

Fig. 6-6. Copyright © Querido. Reproduced by permission of Querido's Uitgeverij

Fig. 6-7. Copyright © Ediciones SM. Reproduced by permission of Ediciones SM

Clothing, as we have just seen, and how it changes throughout time, is also part of the tradition of a country. If we take a look at how our aunty Tante Patent is dressed, we see that this is the way Dutch aunties dressed in the late 60s seen through Fiep Westendorp's eyes. Teresa Novoa dressed her aunty in a more modern way because she did the illustrations for *Tante Patent* in the 90s, although she gave her a classic touch since she told me that aunty Patent reminded her of her History teacher at school. Translation or cultural transplantation is about communication, looking for the effect and making the readers feel closer to the characters in every country, which is what Novoa did.

Something similar happens depicting the grote Sof, the Batavian who becomes the 'vikingo' in Spanish. We know that every country has a different vision or image of a particular referent. Cultural features play an essential role in translation and make a difference. Throughout history, literature, cinema, and television have shaped our idea of what ancient Scandinavian or Germanic warriors looked like and how they behave. Readers will remember well-known viking-like characters such as Vicki the Viking, the superhero Thor from Marvel Comics or Eduardo, a character from Foster's House on Cartoon Network.

As we said, the Viking or Batavian is more than scary: *Sof* is clumsy, funny and rude, but at times he is also sweet and innocent. We might not see all these features reflected in Novoa's Viking, but what we see is the closest image that a Spanish reader would have of a Viking: "As for the Viking, on one hand, he responds to the stereotype we have in Spain of a Viking: tall, big, blond and with a sort of helmet with horns. On the other hand, I used the description in the text to picture him: *Tante Patent wakes up in the middle of the night and thinks that there is a cow in her room.* That is why I drew the Viking with a cow skin sort of dress, with black and white spots", explained Teresa Novoa.

As we see in the illustrations below, however, the *grote Sof* Annie M.G. Schmidt wrote about and that Fiep Westendorp drew was not a Viking but a Batavian, a *batavier*[2]. Novoa 'domesticated' the Batavian, giving him a Viking passport and taking him home, so that Spanish readers would find it easier to identify the character.

Fig. 6-8. Dutch cover. Copyright © Querido. Reproduced by permission of Querido's Uitgeverij

Fig. 6-9. Copyright © Ediciones SM.
Reproduced by permission of Ediciones SM.

As far as their looks are concerned, the Dutch Batavian and the Spanish Viking share many features in common although they also differ in many ways. Looking at all the illustrations dealt with so far, we see that both characters have horns, long hair, moustache or beard, they wear a band around their arms, they are big and strong, they carry a club; they are far removed cousins. It seems that the Dutch Batavian belongs to the wild barbarian side of the family: Fiep Westendorp's Batavian has a more primitive ogre-like appearance; he looks like an animal rather than a man. As a matter of fact, there is an instance (page 10, *Tante Patent*) in which the Batavian's shadow has the shape of a cow. Teresa Novoa's Viking, on the contrary, looks more like a man (and blond, as he is portrayed on the cover of the book). Still, we find the 'cow connection' between the two because the Spanish Viking's dress is made out of cow's skin, to which Teresa Novoa referred to above. The differences in appearance, however, are highly stressed by the fact that through her illustrations, Fiep Westendorp shows us *Sof* behaving in a wider variety of situations and with so many faces that it helps us to create a more complete image of him, to know him better, and hold him dear despite his clumsiness and naughtiness.

Conclusions

All in all, and despite the lack of ambience and humorous mood in the Spanish translation caused by the lack of information and working constraints, Teresa Novoa did an excellent job to the extent she was able to. There are so many differences because they are almost two different stories. It is true that the age of their target readers was the same, but the fact that in the Netherlands and in Spain the book was to be used for different reading objectives, increases the gap between both stories.

We know that adaptation as in modification or adjustment of cultural features for specific reasons is an option. However, publishing houses should realise the importance of the visual in the cultural transfer. Thus, we emphasise the essential role child images and illustrations in general play in communicating thoughts, feelings and values from one culture to another. And we can do this if, as adults, either as parents or as teachers, in Teresa Novoa's words, "we don't see children's books as merely learning-to-read devices; we should consider children's books literary and artistic works that children can like, enjoy, entertain with, and which can teach them aspects of other fields beyond the specific knowledge required in school".

Works Cited

Hervey, Sandor, Ian Higgins and Louise Haywood. *Thinking Spanish Translation*, London & New York: Routledge, 1995.

Schmidt, Annie M.G. *Tante Patent en de grote Sof*, Querido, 1988.

—. *Un vikingo en el jardín*. Translated by Teresa Novoa, Ediciones SM, 1997.

www.annie-mg.nl

www.fiepwestendorp.nl

www.apiv.com/cafe/cafe5/cafes.htm - Gusti's quote was taken from this website which belongs to the Associació Professional d'Il·lustradors de València.

www.lavanguardia.es – Interview to Roser Capdevila, 08/06/2007.

Notes

[1] Adapted from the cline of cultural references in Hervey, Higgins and Haywood (1995: 13).

[2] To be precise from a historical perspective, it is worth mentioning that Batavians (also known as Batavi) were a Germanic tribe, originally part of Chatti, who moved around 100 b.C. from present day Germany to what now is the Netherlands. The Vikings originated in Scandinavia and raided the coasts of the British Isles and mainland Europe as far east as the Volga River in Russia from the late 8th -11th century.

CHAPTER SEVEN

THE RELATIONSHIP BETWEEN TEXT AND ILLUSTRATIONS: TRANSLATING BEATRIX POTTER'S *LITTLE BOOKS* INTO ITALIAN

MARGHERITA IPPOLITO, UNIVERSITY OF BARI

> Visual structures realize meanings as linguistic structures do also, and thereby point to different interpretations of experience and different forms of social interaction. The meanings which can be realized in language and in visual communication overlap in part, that is, some things can be expressed both visually and verbally; and in part they diverge—some things can be "said" only visually, others only verbally.[1]
> —Gunther Kress and Theo van Leeuwen 1996

Introduction

One of the most demanding challenges to the translator's (re)creative abilities are those problems connected with the rendering of the relation between text and illustrations in children's picturebooks. This essay aims to demonstrate that complex narrative interaction between the verbal and visual codes has wide implications for the translation process. A comparative analysis of some tales by Beatrix Potter and their translations into Italian shows that the translator must investigate the different ways in which words and pictures combine together in the source text, in order to organize a coherent target text.

Books with Pictures

Illustrations are a distinctive feature of children's literature. Pictures are an essential medium in comics and picturebooks alike. They also play an important role in other works for children such as pop-up books, fairytales, nursery rhymes, myths, legends, adaptations of Bible stories and novels where, at least on the front cover, pictures of the main characters or events are meant to strike the young reader's attention. Publishers know very well that a book addressed to children without any illustrations has little chance of being noticed or bought. Children are attracted and delighted by images: "[…] what is the use of a book […] without pictures […]?" (Carroll 1865/1992: 10) asks Alice, the main character of Carroll's masterpiece.

The text/image relation is not the same in all children's books. There are some works, such as picturebooks, that inevitably show a marked connection between words and pictures, while there are others that present a weaker tie between the verbal and visual codes, as illustration is merely ornamental, hence of little support to the text.

The Interplay between Words and Pictures

Illustrated storybooks are multimodal systems in which two or more distinct media interact to create highly elaborate language with diversity and homogeneity, contrast and harmony. W.J.T. Mitchell employs the term "imagetexts" (1994: 9) to describe such interaction of the verbal and visual codes and explains that they are "composite synthetic works (or concepts) that combine image and text" (Mitchell 1994: 89). Lawrence Sipe's pivotal concept is "synergy": "In a picture book, both the text and the illustration sequence would be incomplete without the other. They have a synergistic relationship in which the total effect depends not only on the union of the text and illustrations but also on the perceived interactions or transactions between these two parts" (Sipe 1998: 98-99).

The relationship between words and pictures is grounded on a wide range of sophisticated dynamics explored by many scholars. Denise Agosto (1999: 267-280) distinguishes *parallel storytelling*, in which texts and illustrations tell the same story simultaneously, from *interdependent storytelling* in which the reader has to take into consideration both codes in order to understand the plot. Maria Nikolajeva and Carole Scott (2000: 225-239) identify three essential types of text/image relation. *Symmetrical interaction*, where words and pictures provide the same information; *enhancing interaction*, where pictures expand the content of words or the written text enriches the illustration; *counterpoint interaction*, where words and pictures work together to create the meaning of the story.

David Lewis surpasses all those models which pretend to classify the flowing interrelation of text and image rigidly by suggesting a new way of looking at picturebooks: his point is that pictures can repeat, amplify or criticise the story narrated in the text, therefore different types of relationship can coexist within the same book without damaging its unity: "One moment words step forward to occupy centre stage, the next they retire to the wings or comment like a chorus on some key point of the action being played by another part of the text" (Lewis 2001: 52).

Beatrix Potter's Picturebooks

Beatrix Potter's most successful illustrated children's books were written over thirteen years, starting from 1901 with the publication of her first story *The Tale of Peter Rabbit*.

According to Maurice Sendak, Beatrix Potter was "a genius" (1983: xiv). She really had an exceptional natural talent. She was self-taught and when very young, she copied illustrations from books and portrayed animals that she and her brother kept as pets. She later became a regular art gallery visitor and studied the paintings she admired in exhibitions. Indeed, the famous artist John Everett Millais was a close friend of her father's and, although his style is different to Beatrix's, he enlightened her about art. He told her once: "Plenty of people can *draw*, but you and my son John have observation" (Whalley 1987: 47), and with these words he focused on one of Beatrix's greatest gifts: her penetrating observational skill revealed by her scientifically accurate pictures.

Another gift was her way of conveying characters' actions and emotions through pictures alone. Their figurative representation— watercolour being her favourite medium—is provided with psychological depth. Her characters are anthropomorphised animals who communicate their feelings and intentions through their facial expressions, with their body and their glances. Their liveliness certainly attracts the young reader who readily participates intensely in the events. Illustrations have a deep impact on the interpretation of Beatrix Potter's *Little Books* as, without them, they would be different stories, the plots slender and insignificant. According to Nikolajeva and Scott (2000: 230), in the tales there exists a "complementary relationship" between text and illustrations: "In Beatrix Potter's case we see a very effective balance between pictures and prose that complement and enhance one another. They rarely overlap, but rather work together to strengthen the ultimate effect."

The Tale of Mr. Jeremy Fisher (1906) offers a good example of this type of relationship. Jeremy has been prickled by a fish with a thorny back. The narrator says: "And while Mr. Jeremy Fisher sat disconsolately on the edge of his boat—sucking his sore fingers and peering down into the water—a *much* worse thing happened; a really *frightful* thing it would have been, if Mr. Jeremy had not been wearing a macintosh!". (Potter 2002: 127) The text does not reveal the terrible thing that is happening to the main character, but the illustration reveals the mystery. Under the lily leaf upon which Mr. Jeremy Fisher is sitting, the awesome outline of a big fish can be seen approaching dangerously. The tension between the pictures and the text allows the reader to solve the little puzzle, proposed by the verbal code, by looking for clues in the visual one. This apparent discrepancy between the information conveyed by either medium establishes a cohesive force which warns the reader in advance of the imminent danger, the "big fish" in this case.

Fig. 7-1. Illustration from *The Tale of Mr. Jeremy Fisher* by Beatrix Potter, p. 127. Copyright © Frederick Warne & Co., 1903, 2002. Reproduced by permission of Frederick Warne & Co.

The complementary relationship between words and pictures in Potter's tales is not the only dynamic. Magdalena Sikorska, in an essay about Beatrix Potter's picturebooks, points out that: "The reader/viewer finds the storylines overlapping in some passages, while in others the verbal and the visual strands diverge [...]. In the fragments in which the text is dramatic or ambiguous, the visual story is certainly not." (2005: 7)

Translating Picturebooks

Usually, translators cannot modify illustrations. They can intervene only on the verbal text but, at the same time, they must not overlook any interactive influence between the verbal and visual codes.

The translation of picturebooks is a form of "medium-constrained translation", as "neither element—words or pictures—can be isolated, nor are they isolated when the translator translates." (O'Sullivan 2006: 114) The visual and verbal narrative converge to create a unified and integrated whole that must be taken into consideration in its global complexity by the translator. A translation activity limited to the verbal narrative alone would resemble the worst of word by word translation, ignoring the situational or cultural contexts. Inconsistencies and misunderstandings would inevitably spoil the work: "Text and illustrations cannot be separated. Illustrations affect the reader's response and may even guide [his/her] interpretation. By attempting to make text and illustration match, the translator extends [his/her] activities to the illustrations themselves" (Oittinen 1990: 168).

The interplay between text and pictures is a particular challenge to the translator, who has to understand and interpret their relationship. When illustrations only represent what is described in the text and add nothing else to the story, the translator inevitably focuses primarily on the verbal dimension. Instead, when the relation between words and pictures is elaborate the translator's task becomes far more demanding and complex. Special iconotextual reading skills will be required to infer from the picture the atmosphere animating the plot, feelings conveyed by characters' expressions, the setting which may reveal a precise historical period, place or culture. "The pictures stimulate the creative linguistic power of the translator" (O'Sullivan 2006: 114), because she can visualise a character's physical appearance, see the background against which characters act and know what things are supposed to look like. Illustrations give hints as to how to translate, as they provide the translator with all those clues to help choose the right word, fit for the case in hand.

Federico Zanettin, in an essay about the translation of comics, asserts that translators should develop specific text analysis skills, to enable them to consider picturebooks as multidimensional texts, in which linguistic signs are only one component of the communication process Zanettin 1998: 6), therefore, translators should understand the language of illustrations. This language is endowed with a symbolic use of colours and with a series of codes: position (i.e. main characters centrally-placed, secondary ones on fringe); size (i.e. close-up pictures involve reader in narrative, distanced figures make reader feel detached from events); perspective (character placed on two-dimensional plane does not have same inner depth as one portrayed three-dimensionally); line (i.e. angles or boldness suggest danger or emotive tension) (Moebius 1986: 141-158).

The translator must always be aware that the language of illustrations may vary from culture to culture. The challenge to avoid cultural conflictuality in the target language which may arise from a different perception of a given visual item in the source culture, or even mediate the inexistent, is huge.

Beatrix Potter's Tales in Italian

A comparative analysis of the treatment of the iconotextual relationship in translation follows. Three passages from Beatrix Potter's tales with their Italian translations by Giulia Niccolai, who translated only six tales in 1981[2], and by Donatella Ziliotto and Rosalba Ascorti, whose translations were published in 1988 and are still in print[3], will be taken into consideration.

The translations examined will address: (1) how over-explicitation of details present in an illustration may ruin the tension between the verbal and the visual, (2) how simplification of a narrative text may undermine coherence with the illustration; (3) how close scrutiny of the pictures themselves can help to translate far more accurately and appropriately.

In *The Story of A Fierce Bad Rabbit* (1906), an aggressive rabbit assails a good one and steals its carrot. While it is eating the carrot quietly sitting on a bench, a hunter comes up unexpectedly and shoots at it. The double spread is as follows:

But this is all he finds on the bench, when he rushes up with his gun.

Fig.7-2. Illustration from *The Story of A Fierce Bad Rabbit* by Beatrix Potter, p. 138. Copyright © Frederick Warne & Co., 1903, 2002. Reproduced by permission of Frederick Warne & Co.

The deictic *this* refers to the situational context represented in the picture. It directs the reader's attention to the illustration and establishes an interdependence between the verbal and visual strands, as the text cannot be understood without the picture. The omission of certain elements in the written text stimulates the reader to connect both media in order to investigate the meaning of the narrative.

Rosalba Ascorti's translation is:

> Ma quando il cacciatore arriva di corsa, con il fucile in mano, non trova altro che una carota e una coda all'insù. (Ascorti, p. 138)

> But when the hunter rushes up, holding his gun, he finds nothing but a carrot and an upturned tail. (My backtranslation)

The translator fills the gap between written and visual text by making some elements explicit. The position of the hunter's gun and, above all, the carrot and the tail, seen only in the pictures in the source text, are mentioned explicitly in the translated text. Perhaps the translator thinks that the reader is not able to understand this word/image relationship and consequently denies the reader any delight in discovering the details by her/himself and does away with the whole reason for the existence of the visual.

In *The Tale of Squirrel Nutkin* (1903), the main character plays happily while all the other squirrels are looking for food. One of his favourite games is described in one spread:

The other squirrels hunted up and down the nut bushes; but Nutkin gathered robin's pin-cushions off a briar bush, and stuck them full of pine-needle pins.

Fig. 7-3. Illustration from *The Tale of Squirrel Nutkin* by Beatrix Potter, p. 30. Copyright © Frederick Warne & Co., 1903, 2002. Reproduced by permission of Frederick Warne & Co.

Beatrix Potter reproduces with scientific accuracy the form and the colours of robin's pincushions. They look round and hairy on a thorny briar bush. Nutkin is holding one between his paws. The Italian translations are:

> Gli altri scoiattoli facevano man bassa tra i noccioli, ma Nutkin raccolse le bacche pelose di un cespuglio di rose selvatiche e vi piantò degli aghi di pino. (Ziliotto, p. 30)

> The other squirrels hoarded nuts from the hazel bushes, but Nutkin gathered hairy berries off a wild rose bush and stuck pine-needles into them. (My backtranslation)

> Gli altri scoiattoli raccolsero noccioline dai cespugli di nocciole, ma Nocciolina raccolse bacche rosse da un cespuglio di pungitopo e le infilzò tutte con degli aghi di pino. (Giulia Niccolai, p. 37)

> The other squirrels gathered nuts from the hazel bushes, but Nutkin gathered red berries from a butcher's broom bush and stuck pine-needles into all of them. (My backtranslation)

Both translators refuse to translate "robin's pincushions" into Italian, maybe because they think that the literal translation of such scientific term would be incomprehensible to Italian children. Ziliotto replaces "robin's pincushions" with "berries", but since their surface is generally smooth, she adds the adjective "hairy" with the intention of making her translation and the illustration match each other. Niccolai substitutes "robin's pincushions" with "red berries" and "briar bush" with "butcher's broom bush". Her translation choice creates a marked divergence between the verbal text and the illustration. The butcher's broom with its large red berries similar to cherries has nothing in common with the plant represented in the illustration.

In *The Tale of Tom Kitten* (1907), the cats Moppet and Mittens wear lovely pinafores with buttons down the back. Before climbing on to a wall they decide to wear their pinafores back to front in order to be freer in their movements. The illustration supports the text, as it represents the verbal description faithfully:

"Let us climb up the rockery, and sit on the garden wall," said Moppet.

They turned their pinafores back to front, and went up with a skip and a jump.

Fig. 7-4. Illustration from *The Tale of Tom Kitten* by Beatrix Potter, p. 153. Copyright © Frederick Warne & Co., 1903, 2002. Reproduced by permission of Frederick Warne & Co.

The Italian translations go like this:

"Arrampichiamoci sulle rocce e andiamo a sederci sul muro del giardino!" propose Moppet. Rivoltarono i grembiuli, in modo che le macchie non si vedessero, e salirono a balzi e a salti. (Ziliotto, p. 153)

"Let's climb the rocks and go and sit on the garden wall!" proposed Moppet. They turned their pinafores inside out, so the spots could not be seen, and climbed up skipping and jumping. (My backtranslation)

"Perché non scaliamo il giardino di rocce e non ci sediamo sul muretto?", propose Moppet. Si tolsero e si rimisero i grembiulini al contrario e con un balzo e un salto salirono sul muretto. (Niccolai, p. 26)

"Why don't we climb the rockery and sit on the wall?", proposed Moppet. They took their pinafores off and put them on again back to front and with a skip and a jump they climbed the wall. (My backtranslation)

Ziliotto ignores the illustration which clarifies the reasons why the kittens turn their pinafores round, and finds a new justification for their behaviour which is added in the translation: they got dirty while playing and now they want to hide the spots on their pinafores. Any text/image interplay is missing in this translation, because what is told in the verbal narrative finds no correspondence in the visual one and, moreover, the reader cannot see why Moppet and Mittens want to keep their pinafores clean. Niccolai pays attention to the illustration where she finds all the clues necessary to understand the real movements of the kittens. She chooses words that express their actions more closely and the resulting translation is perfectly in tune with the image.

Conclusions

Picturebooks stimulate children to have an interactive role in the reading activity. They encourage them to participate in the verbal and visual interplay as they discover, little by little, all the interweaving pictorial, emotional and narrative strands.

The translator has to unlock the semiotic complexity of a picturebook, in order to recreate the same thing in the target language. By doing so, s/he will avoid concentrating on the verbal strand alone, for picturebooks, after all, propose a multifaceted sensory experience:

> A book *is* more than just something to read … it's something that you want to touch. And when you're designing and binding books, this awareness certainly affects your work: that just the touch and smell and *hold* of a book, is as much part of the pleasure in reading it as is anything else. Especially with kids, who don't lose the pleasure of sensuous experiences, who enjoy touching and feeling and smelling. (Sendak 1983: xix)

Works Cited

Primary Sources of Beatrix Potter's Works Consulted

Potter, Beatrix. *The Complete Tales*. London: Frederick Warne & Co., 2002.

—. *Il mondo di Beatrix Potter*. Translated by Donatella Ziliotto, Rosalba Ascorti, Hado Lyria & Elena Malossini. Milano: Sperling & Kupfer, 2002.

—. *La favola dello scoiattolo Nocciolina*. Translated by Giulia Niccolai. Milano: Emme Edizioni, 1981.

—. *La favola di Tom Miciozzino*. Translated by Giulia Niccolai. Milano: Emme Edizioni, 1981.

Secondary Sources

Agosto, Denise. "One and Inseparable: Interdependent Storytelling in Picture Storybooks." *Children's Literature in Education* 30, no.4 (1999): 267-280.

Carroll, Lewis. *Alice's Adventures in Wonderland* (1865). London; New York: Norton, 1992.

Kress, Gunther and Theo van Leeuwen. *Reading Images. The Grammar of Visual Design*. London; New York: Routledge, 1996.

Lewis, David. *Reading Contemporary Picturebooks: Picturing Text*. London; New York: Routledge, 2001.

Mitchell, W. J. T. *Picture Theory: Essays on Verbal and Visual Representation*. Chicago: University of Chicago Press, 1994.

Moebius, William. "Introduction to Picturebook Codes." *Word & Image* 2, no. 2 (1986): 141-158.

Nikolajeva, Maria and Carole Scott. "The Dynamics of Picturebook Communication." *Children's Literature in Education*, 31, no. 4 (2000): 225-239.

Oittinen, Riitta. "The Dialogic Relation between Text and Illustration: A Translatological View." *TextconText* 5, no. 1 (1990): 40-53.

O'Sullivan, Emer. "Translating Pictures." In *The Translation of Children's Literature. A Reader*, Gillian Lathey, 113-121. Clevedon: Multilingual Matters, 2006.

Sendak, Maurice. "A Dialogue with Maurice Sendak." In *Victorian Color Picture Books*, edited by Jonathan Cott, ix-xxi. New York: Stonehill Publishing Company in association with Chelsea House, 1983.

Sikorska, Magdalena. "The Stories Illustrations Tell: The Creative Illustrating Strategy in the Pictures by Beatrix Potter and Janosch." *New Review of Children's Literature and Librarianship* 11, no. 1 (2005): 1-14.

Sipe, Lawrence R. "How Picture Books Work: A Semiotically Framed Theory of Text-Picture Relationships." *Children's Literature in Education* 29, no. 2 (1998): 97-108.

Whalley, Joyce Irene. "The Young Artist and the Early Influence." In *Beatrix Potter 1866-1943. The Artist and her World*, edited by Judy Taylor, Joyce Irene Whalley, Anne Stevenson Hobbs & Elizabeth M. Battrick, 35-48. London: Warne, 1987.

Zanettin, Federico. "Fumetti e traduzione multimediale. Tra codice verbale e codice visivo." *InTRAlinea* 1 (1998): 1-7. http://www.intralinea.it/volumes/ita_more.php?id=156_0_2_0_C (accessed November 19, 2007).

Notes

[1] Kress and van Leeuwen, *Reading Images. The Grammar of Visual Design*, 2.

[2] Giulia Niccolai translated *The Tale of Peter Rabbit*, *The Tale of Squirrel Nutkin*, *The Tale of Benjamin Bunny*, *The Tale of Tom Kitten*, *The Tale of Jeremy Fisher*, *The Tale of Mrs. Tiggy-Winkle*. They were published by Emme Edizioni in Milan.

[3] Sperling & Kupfer have published all Potter's tales in Italian. The little books were translated by Donatella Ziliotto, Rosalba Ascorti, Hado Lyria and Elena Malossini. Each of them translated a different tale.

CHAPTER EIGHT

CHANGES AND EXCHANGES: VARIATIONS IN THE ILLUSTRATIONS IN TRANSLATED CHILDREN'S LITERATURE

MARTIN B. FISCHER, UNIVERSITY POMPEU FABRA

Introduction

In this paper I will present some translations of Austrian writer Christine Nöstlinger's books into Spanish and Catalan, with special emphasis on the illustrations. Some of her books have been illustrated by the author, her daughters (Barbara Waldschütz, Christi(a)ne Nöstlinger jr.) or other well-known artists. Not all of the translated books maintain the illustrations of the German language editions: they may have new illustrations or none.

First, there will be given an overview of several of the Spanish and Catalan editions of Nöstlinger's novels for children and young people and then we will centre our attention on the book *Das Austauschkind / Intercambio con un inglés* [Exchange With an English Boy] analysing the illustrations in the first Austrian edition and the Spanish edition, and trying to explain what could have motivated some of the possible changes and commenting the different styles of the artists.

Christine Nöstlinger

The Austrian writer Christine Nöstlinger (Vienna 1936)[1] wrote more than 80 books for children and young people, a lot of which have been translated into other European languages. In Spain there are translations into all the four official languages of the State, i.e. Spanish, Catalan, Basque and Galician.

Nöstlinger, who studied graphical design, published her first book with her own illustrations: *Die feuerrote Friederike* (1970). The new edition of the book in German (1996) was illustrated by the author's daughter, Barbara Waldschütz; both translations (Catalan 1996; Spanish 1997) use those illustrations. The German and Austrian editions of many of her books have been illustrated by renowned artists, such as Janosch, Jutta Bauer, Edith Schindler, F.K. Waechter, Karin Schubert, Nikolaus Heidelbach and others.

Nöstlinger's early books may be classified as typical for critical realism (*Ilse Janda, 14* 1974, *Der Spatz in der Hand* 1974). Later, she developed her own, humoristic style, characterized by the frequent use of irony, puns and creative neologisms (composed nouns). Among her works there are to find classic titles of anti-authoritarian children's literature (*Wir pfeifen auf den Gurkenkönig* 1972, *Konrad oder Das Kind aus der Konservendose* 1975), but also satires (*Rüb, rüb, hurra!* 1975), easy to read series for young children (*Susi, Mini* and *Franz*), books about the emancipation of girls (*Rosalinde hat Gedanken im Kopf* 1980) and books for teenagers, about family problems and personal identity (*Gretchen Sackmeier* 1981, *Olfi Obermeier und der Ödipus* 1984 or *Bonsai* 1997). Some of her books have an autobiographical background: *Maikäfer flieg* (1973), *Zwei Wochen im Mai* (1981) or *Der geheime Großvater* (1986).

The Importance and the Role of Illustrations

Although many, if not all, texts allow and maybe even demand new illustrations from time to time, there are books which are related to the pictures of one artist, such as John Tenniel's illustrations for *Alice's Adventures in Wonderland* or Aubrey Beardsley's for Oscar Wilde's *Salomé*. A modern example of this symbiotically empathic relationship between the author and the illustrator in children's literature would be Roald Dahl and Quentin Blake. In German Children's Literature, I would like to name the duo Erich Kästner and Walter Trier. Surely all of us remember certain books we have read in our childhood, first for their illustrations and then for the text (cf. Fischer 2006, chap. 7).

Of course there are authors who illustrate their own books, too. Just think of Saint-Exupéry's *Le petit prince*. This was also the case of Heinrich Hoffmann who wrote and drew Germany's most famous and discussed picture book, *Der Struwwelpeter*. In contemporary German literature, we could mention Günter Grass and, in children's literature, Janosch or Jutta Bauer.

Illustrations always have multiple functions:
a) Creativity. First of all, they are the genuine expression of an artist's creativity and his/her interpretation of the text.
b) Interaction. They interact with the text and its message. See what British artist John Vernon Lord points out: "The main function of the children's book illustrator is to represent, interpret, and heighten the meaning of a text (in a complementary way) by means of pictures, with the aim of bringing life to a story" (Lord 1997: 83).[2]
c) Alternative readings. Frequently, illustrations offer an alternative reading to complete and contrast the text.
d) Intertextuality. As the text itself, they can allude to other texts or images.
e) Emotional dimension. Illustrations also contribute to the humorous or any other emotional dimension of the text: they may enforce its comical power or even create comical issues which were not evident in the text itself.
f) Contemporary norms. Illustrations usually reflect current artistic norms, trends and tastes.
g) Last but not least, they may offer information about the cultural context: show traditional houses, clothes, meals etc. Information of that sort may be of special interest for translators because it helps them to understand ambiguous or obscure parts of the text.

In Nöstlinger's *Lollipop* (1977) illustrator Angelika Kaufmann shows a typical backyard (*Hinterhof*) of German and Austrian 19th century urban flat buildings. The drawing (as all the other illustrations) also appears in the Spanish and Catalan editions of the book and thus makes it easier for readers to understand the text which describes the view out of a kitchen window in the rear part of the building (cf. Fischer 1999 and 2000).

On the other hand, if the illustrations are to be taken over in the translated book and carry a big burden of culture items (such as everyday life issues), they may cause some difficulty for the translator, who will not feel free to adapt certain details to the target culture.

This is also the point where illustration as a subject becomes part of the more fundamental discussion about what the task or role of children's literature is supposed to be in first place: mere pleasure or educational tool – or both. Here the question would be whether a story situated in Germany or Austria could or should be adapted to the cultural context of the target language, domesticated[3] or even transferred to Spain or Catalonia or, on the contrary, whether the translation could or should show the target readers the (supposed) reality of the countries where the story originally happens.

If a translated book is to be published with the illustrations of the original book, there are a lot of issues to be taken in account:

a) Are the rights available? Will the production be profitable? (colour or black-and-white)

b) Will readers in the target country like the illustrations in the book?

c) Do they fit in the line of characteristic illustrations the publishing house (if there are any)?

d) Could there be any problems because of non-politically correct illustrations?[4]

e) Are the illustrations up-to-date or démodé?

f) If the translation adapts completely or up to a certain degree – are the illustrations still congruent with the text?

New illustrations, on the contrary, obviously give editors a greater autonomy and may allow for an independent dialogue between the illustrator and the translated text, comparable to the relation between the author and the illustrator of the original.

Among the translations of Christine Nöstlinger's books in Spain there are all sort of solutions: using the same presentation and lay-out as the German editions, or translations without the illustrations of the original editions and editions with new illustrations. See some examples:

a) Same size, same lay-out/presentation and same illustrations (only the text is changed):
Der Neue Pinocchio, Weinheim/Basel, 1988, colour illustrations by Nikolaus Heidelbach, *El Nuevo Pinocho*, Valencia, 1988; colour illustrations by Nikolaus Heidelbach, transl. Manuel Ramírez Giménez, *El Nou Pinotxo*, Valencia, 1988; colour illustrations by Nikolaus Heidelbach, transl. Heike Van Lawick Brozio and Vicent Pascual.

b) Different illustrations, similar size (see section 3 of this article): *Das Austauschkind*, Viena, 1982, *Intercambio con un inglés*, Madrid, 1986.

c) Different illustrations, different size: *Madisou*: Christine Nöstlinger and Frank Abu Sidibé, Vienna, 1995, almost DIN A4 (21x29 cm), colour illustrations by Barbara Waldschütz, *Madisú*: Christine Nöstlinger and Frank Abu Sidibé, transl. Edda Monika

Brughardt, Madrid, 1997, 13 x 18,5 cm, colour illustrations by
Arnal Ballester.

d) Illustrations in the German books and no illustrations in the
translations: Spanish translation of *Der geheimnisvolle Großvater*,
1986 (*El abuelo misterioso*, 1990); Catalan translations of *Oh du
Hölle!* – *Julias Tagebuch*, 1986 (*El diari de Júlia*, 1989) or *Der
Zwerg im Ohr*, 1989 (*El follet ficat al cap*, 1995).

The most interesting cases are actually those in which new illustrations
substitute the "original" ones. Usually, we may only speculate about
reasons for changes concerning the illustrations. In the case of *Der liebe
Herr Teufel / El simpàtic senyor Dimoni* (also in Spanish and Basque) it
seems quite obvious that the temporal distance between the first
publication of the German text (1975) and the translations (1999) has
motivated new illustrations: the tiny ink-drawings of Peter Giesel didn't fit
in modern Catalan publishing policy, so Pep Montserrat created vigorous
colour paintings that confer to the adapted text a contemporary touch.

Fig. 8-1. *El simpàtic senyor Dimoni*, illustration by Pep Montserrat. © 1999.
Permission granted by Editorial Cadí.

The same reason – drawings that are considered to be old-fashioned–
may have motivated the decision to publish the Catalan translation of *Wir
pfeifen auf den Gurkenkönig* (1972), *Cop d'escombra al rei Cogombre*
(1992), without the original drawings by Werner Maurer. In the year of the
first publication, however, those illustrations–and the text, of course!–
could have easily been considered politically incorrect in some countries

(e.g., a boy playing with a doll's pram). Interestingly enough, the Spanish translation of 1984 offers Maurer's drawings.

Das Austauschkind

The story

In *Das Austauschkind* by Christine Nöstlinger, a thirteen-year-old boy from Vienna, Ewald Mittermeier, tells the readers all about what happens to him and his family before the arrival and during the stay of Jasper, an English boy on an exchange visit, in their home. The perspective of a (teenage) protagonist is one of the favourite resorts of the author as it allows her to use a colloquial, idiomatic tone, near to young reader's own language.

Jasper is not the boy the Mittermeier family actually expected: he comes instead of his stepbrother Tom, who had broken his leg. Throughout the book, it becomes clear that Jasper has not only very bad manners but also that he is a quite unconventional person who suffers due to the divorce of his parents. A lot of funny and/or tragic situations follow each other.

One of the most comical issues is the non-adequate use of English by Ewald's father, who simply translates his German phrases word-by-word into English; for instance, explaining a photograph, in the letter to the parents of the English boy: "My sister Sybille was taking us up", from "Meine Schwester Sybille hat uns aufgenommen". The verb *aufnehmen* means to take a photograph in German. In the first edition of the book, Christine Nöstlinger jr. draws the letter and the photograph (AKd1, p. 33). The comical dimension of that kind of false phrases can only be appreciated totally by people who understand both, English and German (cf. Fischer 2006: 304-310). Readers of the Spanish translation find a glossary of English words at the end of the book.

The title of the book

The German title–literally "The Exchange Child"–is not very adequate for the protagonist's age (14); the neutral Spanish version–"Exchange with an English [Boy]"–is preferable. The cover design and the illustrations of the first German/Austrian edition nevertheless harmonize with this childlike image. The title of the Basque translation means "An English [boy] in the house".

The cover design

We will compare the first edition in German from 1982, the second, a pocket edition (1995), three Spanish editions and a Basque one. On the cover of the first Vienna edition, a happily smiling Jasper, wearing dark blue sun glasses, is sitting on his suitcase, with an umbrella, a rucksack and some beach toys. This illustration doesn't correspond to any specific scene of the text.

The pocket edition by Beltz & Gelberg (AKd2[5]) shows Ewald, Jasper and Sybille eating *Langosch*, a typical Austro-Hungarian salted pastry filled with garlic sauce, with the giant wheel (*Riesenrad*) in Vienna's *Prater* amusement park in the background. This cover illustration by Axel Scheffler may have been inspired by Nöstlinger jr.'s text illustration (p. 85 AKd1).

For the first Spanish translation, a colour drawing by Amechazurra has been used. It shows Jasper and Ewald on their way back home from the supermarket (where Jasper has been stealing things; illustration p. 97, AKs2). This drawing doesn't appear as a text illustration, neither in this nor in the second edition. The cover of this second edition is a collage with a "modern" look, but without any special relation to the text: a laughing girl standing next to a fair haired boy in a huge armchair can be seen. The cover of the most recent Spanish edition is even less related to the text: three toothbrushes in a glass, although there is a text drawing showing Ewald and Sybille brushing their teeth.

The cover of the Basque translation (AKb, 1991/2000) is a framed, little colour painting, inspired obviously in Amechazurra's drawing from page 77 (AKs2): Ewald's mother shrieks facing nude Jasper. There are no text illustrations in the Basque edition.

Fig. 8-2. *Intercambio con un inglés*, illustration by Gerardo Amechazurra. © 1986.
Permission granted by Espasa Calpe.

The text illustrations

The German text is illustrated with 16 whole page drawings, mostly in the second part of the book, while the Spanish edition counts 20 illustrations, six of which extend over the whole page. In spite of the different cover designs and pagination, the text illustrations of the different Spanish editions don't change.

I have already mentioned above that illustrations may heighten the humorous power of a text. This is the case of Amechazurra's drawings: their caricaturized or even comic-like character make us laugh.

It is eye-opening to read the description of Jasper's arrival at Schwechat Airport and see first the illustration by Christine Nöstlinger jr and then compare it with Amechazurra's illustration of the same scene: "Ein korpulenter, rotblonder, sommersprossiger Knabe stürzte auf das Fließband zu, packte die rote Tasche und den Wandermannsbinkel mit einer Hand und den froschgrünen Koffer mit der anderen und watschelte dem Ausgang und dem Zöllner zu" (p. 44; A corpulent red haired boy with freckles sprang towards the baggage claim belt, took the red bag and the wanderer's bundle with one hand and the frog green suitcase with the other and began walking ducklike towards the exit and the customs control; my translation)

In Nöstlinger jr.'s drawing, Jasper seems to be quite a handsome boy with a lot of luggage, holding in his right hand the photograph Ewald's father sent him to recognize the host family on arrival. If it wasn't for the sarcastic comment of Ewald's class-mate Peter ("For heavens sake! It's Jasper, the devil") we would not expect any harm of the boy. There is just the cloud with a flash of lightning on his T-shirt that may be seen as an ironic hint to Jasper's "stormy" character.

Amechazurra's illustration, on the contrary, already shows the strong personality of the guest: he arrives as an invader who will disturb the homely peace in the house of the Mittermeier family.

Fig. 8-3. *Intercambio con un inglés*, illustration by Gerardo Amechazurra. © 1986. Permission granted by Espasa Calpe.

The Spanish illustrator then offers two little drawings that show us how Ewald has to leave his room for Jasper ("I need a room of my own" p. 55) and how the latter puts lots of ketchup on his meal.

In the next illustration in the German book, Jasper is to be seen naked, with (red) socks on his feet and a leather belt with a knife in its sheath round his waist. He seems to be surprised and a little ashamed because he puts his hand before his mouth (but doesn't hide his sex).

In the Spanish illustration, however, Jasper is shown from behind, at the very moment Ewald's mother is entering the room to take him out of bed (Ewald's father has planned a family trip, at nine o'clock on Sunday morning) (see Fig. 8-2).

The comparison of those two drawings is especially interesting as they are based on the same text passage, yet show totally different solutions. Amechazurra not only takes full advantage of the dramatic power of the scene, but also changes the perspective. We wonder if his decision has to be seen only as a creative resort or if the change has been done to avoid showing Jasper's genitals explicitly, as well. In any case, he leaves to the reader's imagination what Ewald's mother really sees.

Ewald's father starts a brutal re-education of the English boy. The children, first Sybille, Ewald's elder sister, and then Ewald himself protest and make common cause with the guest. As time goes by, the parents nevertheless begin to understand Jasper's strange behaviour as they learn details about his personal story. They all go on holiday together and, finally, even travel to Italy to try and find Jasper's stepmother, the one he loves more than his real mother.

Among the further illustrations in the German book, I would like to mention the one on page 129, which shows Jasper in bed, reading *Finnegan's Wake*. The drawing underlines the intertextual reference present in the text, which is a good example of the author's use of irony, too: "Manchmal las er aber auch in einem Buch, das er mitgebracht hatte. Es hieß *Finnegans Wake* [sic] und war von einem James Joyce. Jasper sagte uns, er verstehe das ganze Buch überhaupt nicht, aber es sei trotzdem wunderschön" (Akd1 97/98; "He sometimes read in a book he had brought with him, called *Finnegans Wake* [sic], written by a certain James Joyce. Jasper told us he didn't understand anything of the book but that, nevertheless, it was just wonderful"). Amechazurra doesn't recreate this intertextual reference in an illustration.

The Spanish book's illustrations don't always refer to the same scenes as those in the German edition. Amechazurra, for instance, doesn't illustrate the *Prater* scene either: he draws Ewald's and Sybille's mother instead, wondering about how a paper flower from the amusement park may have got on the mantelpiece in the family's flat (AKs2, p. 90). In the drawings we don't find any detail that may be considered traditionally Austrian. Luis Pastor, the Spanish translator, tends to generalize the traditional Austrian dishes and pastries and other cultural items: *Schwarzwälder Kirschtorte* (cherry tart Black Forest style with cream and chocolate, AKd2 p. 54) becomes *tarta de cerezas* (cherry tart) (AKs2, 61), *Langosch* (salted pastry, originally from Hungary, AKd2, p. 83) *empanadas* (pasties, AKs2, p. 88). He only maintains *gulasch* (AKs 48). *Prater* (Vienna's famous amusement park) is translated as *Parque de Atracciones* (AKs2, p. 87).

The comparison of the illustrations of the German and the Spanish editions makes it evident that the two artists were free to decide which parts of the text they wanted to illustrate. Although Amechazurra prefers the "dramatic" scenes, we also find drawn comments on every-day life among his illustrations. But Nöstlinger jr.'s illustrations are always "cuter" and more childlike.

Before I come to an end, I would just like to stress this fact with two more drawings. Nöstlinger jr. shows Ewald and his sister buying in the supermarket with a cart (p. 126), an every-day life scene of no further interest. Amechazurra, on the contrary, illustrates a shopping scene which is not mentioned explicitly in the book: Ewald and Jasper, the latter stuffing things in his chest pocket with multiplied arms, like an Indian Goddess, to show his skill (p. 97).

The whole family with the English guest goes on holiday down to Italy. Nöstlinger jr. drew two pictures that show sad, crying Jasper (p. 103 and 117) while Amechazurra shows just one, the most drastic: after having spoken with his beloved stepmother – who doesn't want to see him – (that is the passage Nöstlinger jr. illustrates) he becomes outrageous and throws all his pebbles against the wall of the hotel room: this is the moment chosen by the Spanish artist:

Fig. 8-4. *Intercambio con un inglés*, illustration by Gerardo Amechazurra. © 1986. Permission granted by Espasa Calpe.

The illustrations by Christine Nöstlinger jr. and Gerardo Amechazurra do not only differ in the selection of specific scenes from the text, but also in the technique. Nöstlinger's are plain, static, mostly lacking perspective and kind of mannerist with their love for tiny little details and always well framed, while Amechazurra is best when he creates dynamic situations, seen from different points of view, mostly slightly from beneath, with figures in an imposing attitude and nearly always breaking the drawn frame.

Conclusions

The comparison between the illustrations of the German and the Spanish editions of Christine Nöstlingers's book *Das Austauschkind / Intercambio con un inglés* shows up to what degree illustrators may interpret or heighten the text that inspires them. As the illustrations of the first German edition of the book are made by the author's daughter, one may suppose they had her consent even if they are quite naïve and, therefore, not necessarily appropriate for both the protagonist's and the reader's age. Nöstlinger jr.'s drawings just accompany the text and tend to understate the dramatic and the comical dimension of the text.[6] Although they give the reader some graphical information about Austrian food and other characteristics of everyday life, their main function seems to be just to guarantee a pleasant reading.

Amechazurra's illustrations, on the contrary, not only complement and interpret the translated text, but also heighten its tragicomic power. I therefore think that Amechazurra's drawings suit much better Christine Nöstlinger's ironic style in this book for young people. Luis Pastor's translation succeeds in rendering the author's irony. A certain loss can be observed, however, regarding puns with false "English" phrases.[7] Amechazurra's illustrations help to compensate that loss. Thus their function becomes clear: to offer the reader a complementary view of things to happen and, at the same time, reinforce the inherent characteristics of the text, i.e. underline its emotional dimension.

It has become clear, too, that illustrations depend on changing tastes and fashions as well as many other issues. This is proved, on the one hand, by the *Austauschkind* and other books and their translations mentioned in this article, and on the other hand, by the three different cover designs of the Spanish editions.

Finally, we confirm that illustrating, writing and translating are all creative processes which should complement each other in order to give birth to eye-opening and enjoyable books.

Works Cited

Books by Christine Nöstlinger

Das Austauschkind (1982) Vienna: Verlag Jugend & Volk / Weinheim & Basel: Beltz und Gelberg, 1995. AKd1 / AKd2

Intercambio con un inglés (1986) transl. by Luis Pastor, ill. by Gerardo Amechazurra, Madrid: Espasa-Calpe. AKs (new cover 1997, new cover in the collection "Camaleón" 2004) AKs1

Ingeles bat etxean (1991), transl. by Xabier Mendiguren, Donostia / San Sebastián: Elkar. Akb

Der liebe Herr Teufel (1975), ill. by Peter Giesel, Vienna: Jugend und Volk; also rororo, 1977.

El simpàtic senyor Dimoni (1999), ill. by Pep Montserrat, transl. by Georgina Castellà i Fernàndez, Barcelona: Cadí.

Lollipop (1977), ill. by Angelika Kaufmann, Weinheim und Basel: Beltz & Gelberg, 1986.

Piruleta (1984) ill. by Angelika Kaufmann, transl. by Mario García Aldonate, Madrid: Alfaguara.

Lollipop (1993) ill. by Angelika Kaufmann, transl. by Antoni Arrufat, Barcelona: Alfaguara.

Wir pfeifen auf den Gurkenkönig. Wolfgang Hogelmann erzählt die Wahrheit, ohne auf die Deutschlehrergliederung zu verzichten, Ein Kinderroman (1977) ill. by Werner Maurer, Reinbek bei Hamburg: Rowohlt (Weinheim und Basel: Beltz 1972).

Me importa un comino el rei Pepino (1984) transl. by María Jesús Ampudia, ill. by Werner Maurer, Madrid: Alfaguara.

Cop d'escombra al Rei Cogombre (1992) transl. by Sylvia Halm, cover design by Enric Casassas Figueres, Barcelona: Empúries.

Madisou: Christine Nöstlinger and Frank Abu Sidibé, Vienna: Dachs, 1995, colour illustrations by Barbara Waldschütz

Madisú: Christine Nöstlinger and Frank Abu Sidibé, transl. by Edda Monika Brughardt, Madrid: Ediciones Gaviota, 1997.

Der Neue Pinocchio, ill. Nikolaus Heidelbach, Weinheim/Basel: Beltz & Gelberg, 1988.

El Nuevo Pinocho, ill. Nikolaus Heidelbach, transl. by Manuel Ramírez Giménez, Valencia: Mestral, 1988.

El Nou Pinotxo, ill. Nikolaus Heidelbach, transl. by Heike Van Lawick Brozio / Vicent Pascual, Valencia: Gregal, 1988.

On children's literature and illustrations

Colomer, Teresa. "Texto, imagen, imaginación". In *CLIJ* 130, September, (2000): 7-17.

Fernández López, Marisa. "Canon y periferia en la literatura infantil y juvenil: manipulación del medio visual". In Lorenzo / Pereira / Ruzicka (eds.) *Contribuciones al estudio de la traducción de literatura infantil y juvenil*, Madrid: Dossat 2000, 2002, (2002): 13-42.

Fischer, Martin B. "Hinterhof und Powidltatschkerln. Kulturspezifika bei der Übersetzung von Kinderliteratur". In *Grenzgänge* 11, (1999): 62-81 (also: www.ucm.es/info/especulo/ele/vigo.html)

—. "Diferencias culturales reflejadas en la Literatura Infantil y Juvenil". In Ruzicka Kenfel / Vázquez García / Lorenzo García (eds.) *Literatura infantil y juvenil: tendencias actuales en investigación*, Universidade de Vigo, (2000): 149-160.

—. *Konrad und Gurkenkönig jenseits der Pyrenäen*. Frankfurt/M.: Peter Lang, 2006.

Lord, John Vernon. "Some aspects of what an illustrator has to think about when creating children's picture books". In Duran, Teresa (ed.) *IV Simposi Premi Internacional CATALÒNIA d'Il·lustració*, Barcelona: Enciclopèdia Catalana (Script), (1997): 83-90.

Notes

[1] Nöstlinger received the Hans Christian Andersen Prize in 1984 and the Astrid-Lindgren-Prize in 2003.

[2] See also Colomer, Teresa 2000.

[3] See Fischer 2006, chapter 4.7, pp. 152-163, especially 155.

[4] See, for instance, Fernández López 2002, pp. 32-33.

[5] See bibliography: "AKd2" means *Das Austauschkind* pocket edition, Weinheim & Basel: Beltz und Gelberg 1995.

[6] It is possible that the infantile character of Nöstlinger jr.'s drawings motivated the editors of some Catalan versions of her mother's novels for young people not to include them, while the books for younger children–like the *Susi* or *Mini* series–do reproduce them. They also fit well in teenage Julia's diary in *Oh du Hölle*, Beltz & Gelberg, 1986.

[7] For more details on this issue, see Fischer 2007: 304-310.

PART IV:

TEACHING AND READING LITERATURE FOR YOUNG READERS IN TRANSLATION

CHAPTER NINE

FAIRY TALE RETELLINGS AS TRANSLATION: DEVELOPING VERBAL AND VISUAL INTERCULTURAL COMPETENCE

MARIA GONZÁLEZ DAVIES, UNIVERSITY RAMON LLULL

> We know now that a text is not a line of words releasing a single "theological" meaning (the message of the Author-God) but a multidimensional space in which a variety of writings, none of them an original, blend and clash. The text is a tissue of quotations drawn from the innumerable centres of culture.
> —Roland Barthes 1977

Introduction

Straightforward translations are easily identifiable but, what about retellings of folk and fairy tales? Can they be considered and studied as verbal and visual translations? Can they be analyzed in a similar way to translations and help improve intercultural competence in educational contexts? Both fairy tale retellings and new translations of the same text display new norms related to a receiving community or generation that need to construct new identities and often do so through selecting, interpreting and reconstructing earlier texts. These retellings and retranslations can be viewed as total or partial verbal and visual transplantations adapted–or not–to the receiving readers. If, following Jakobson's classification of translations (1959/1971), fairy tale retellings are also examined as intralinguistic, interlinguistic or intersemiotic translations, they then become eye-opening material to develop intra and intercultural competence.

To illustrate how theoretical sensitising can initiate practical classroom procedures, I will present a selection of some of the most relevant outcomes of a pilot project carried out with my Teacher Training students at Blanquerna (University Ramon Llull). The aims were to raise awareness of these issues as well as to explore the potential of presenting fairy tale retellings as a valuable learning procedure to favour the development of both their own and their future students' intra and intercultural competence. The project, which revolved around research related to the tale *Cinderella*, is transferable to other educational levels and contexts.

Fairy tales, translation and intercultural competence

By its very nature, translation is related to intercultural competence. By transmission processes, fairy tales have spread to different cultures. Therefore, why not establish a dialogue between these fields to develop intra and intercultural competence in different educational contexts? Intercultural competence here is defined as the ability to understand different value systems significantly and behave appropriately in more than one community. The working framework is far from definitions of "stable culture" and near to a notion of culture as a fluctuating feature of human relationships: the same person can "belong" to different communities in his or her lifetime, thus reshaping his or her identity. This definition can be extended to that of intracultural competence when applied to one's own communit(ies). In our globalized world, intercultural competence has become one of the main competences expected from present and future generations to cope with the new social and economic challenges.[1] It is at the core of recent processes of most educational reforms[2], all of which makes fairy tale[3] retellings, studied from an intercultural angle specially relevant in different academic subjects such as Literature, Foreign Language Acquisition or Translation. Myths and fairy tales are a common background to most cultures that work on many levels and invite many angles of interpretation. They form a body of accessible sources (from books to the Internet) that include subject matters common to many communities. This makes it possible for mental and emotional associations to be quickly established and can open paths towards mutual understanding. However, their effective study in different subjects entails sensitising the students by creating an awareness of

a) the existence of different versions in different cultures and different generations,
b) how the versions reflect the sociohistorical and psychological value systems of the communities and generations that produced them, and
c) the fact that these versions include both verbal and visual changes.

By connecting with versions of the same tale as told in different communities in different periods, children and adults can develop their critical thinking skills and become aware of issues that may put into perspective and raise questions related to their own cultural and generational standpoints, reflect on the need to respect those of others and understand about the relativity of all viewpoints, thus learning to notice similarities and celebrate diversity. This leads to enhanced intercultural awareness related to collective and individual value systems when choosing texts to read–or to be read in the case of adults for children.

Translation studies and fairy tale retellings

To translate, *trans-ducere*, to take somewhere else *externally*, in space and time... To be emotive, *e-movere*, to move somewhere else *internally*, in space and time...

Through retellings and translations, one is moved, trans-ported according to literary and translatory norms. The well-known didactic intention of fairy tales since their origins has stressed their two main functions: to depict both existing or desired sociohistorical and psychological contexts. These two functions have had their echo in critical approaches to their study, such as the social realistic, psychoanalytical or fantasy interpretations. They can become, in Joosen's words, "instruments of social acculturation" (2005: 219) where lessons on different issues are put forward: gender, social advancement, accepted behaviours, and so on. Translators usually operate between imposed constraints and subjective idiosincracies reflecting the social and historical trends of the target community in their choices. Alongside the community's search for identity, individual processes of individuation are triggered in constant interaction: this brings about changes in different degrees, reflected in its (translated) literature.

Translation Studies can offer interesting means to observe and analyse the intercultural and intergenerational aspects that appear in fairy tale retellings. The tension between source text and target text here really means the tension between (linguistic, geographical or generational) source and target cultures and norms, between past and present external and internal identity-shaping forces. Since the 1980s, Translation Studies have moved forward from constrictive evaluations based almost exclusively on Contrastive Linguistics and a philological and hermeneutic outlook, to approaches including cultural studies, cognitive psychology and functionalism. Let us see briefly how some of the main theories and approaches can be relevant when exploring fairy tale retellings in different educational contexts:

Fairy tales and translations have mainly been perceived as non-canonical–peripheral–in most communities. With postcolonial studies and deconstruction, however, canons have been reconsidered. Specially relevant has been Even-Zohar's (1990) and Toury's Polysystems theory, which has done much to do away with prejudices and open new paths of research (for an updated interpretation, see Tymoczko 2000). In Toury's words (1995: 53):

> Translation activities should rather be regarded as having cultural significance. Consequently, 'translatorship' amounts first and foremost to being able to *play a social role*, i.e., to fulfil a function allotted by a community–to the activity, its practitioners and/or their products–in a way which is deemed appropriate in its own terms of reference.

The main idea is that a community is an addition of fluctuating systems (literary, political, religious, etc.) and that these systems conform to norms, traditional or innovative. Primary (non-canonical) texts are in constant struggle against secondary (canonical) texts for the dominant position. Interestingly, translation has very often operated as an active agent of transformation by introducing new verbal and visual material which has become secondary in the system.

Cultural Studies in Translation–the *cultural turn*–have also been a turning point in perceptions of the translator's task, especially that of the literary translator. Bahktin's dialogue and carnival have been taken further by studies on the translator's visibility (Venuti 1995), and gender, frontera, or cannibalistic theories of translation. Literary translations are now generally considered as re-creations, whether they conform to or rebel against the target culture's rules. In Berman's words:

> Translation [...] is about lies and truth, betrayal and fidelity; about mimesis, doubleness, illusion, secondarity; about the life of the meaning and the life of the setter; thinking about it is to be caught up in an inebriating reflexive whirlwind where even the word 'translation' endlessly metaphorizes itself. (Berman, in Nouss 2001: 283).

Also relevant to our topic is Functionalism and its assertion that the initiator is the key agent that triggers the translation process (Nord 1997). The perspective of the new text or illustrations can change considerably depending on whether the initiator is the translator or a publishing house, for instance. It may establish the difference between conforming to or challenging the receiving culture's norms, or between keeping the illustrations of the source text or consigning new ones, or even whether the illustrator will read the text before starting to work (see Español, Fischer, Oittinen in this volume).

In literary translations, then, two forces act: the individual translator's competence and subjectivity as well as the application of the accepted social and, so, translational, norms of his or her time. When tackling a translation, the translator fuses these two forces and interprets, re-tells, the source story. This can be done consciously or unconsciously. Something similar happens with the illustrator. Words and illustrations combine to create a world that is not completely new, but which looks at the source world from a different angle, distorted if the illustrations have not followed the variations in the translated or retold text.

The observation and study of translation competence occupies a central place in these new approaches to translation studies. There are quite a few proposals to explain how the translator's mind works, most of which can be summarised as the need to acquire appropriate *aptitudes*, that is, interlinguistic, encyclopaedic and transferential skills, on the one hand, and *attitude*, that is, mainly professional skills, self-concept, motivation and subjectivity, on the other (González Davies 2004: 131, 217).

Finally, translation teaching has also evolved over the past decade into a varied and complex subfield of translation studies. There are three major reasons for this trend: (1) advances in translation theory, (2) the application of findings from educational research to the teaching of professional translation skills, and (3) the advent of the personal computer and related technologies as essential tools for professional translators. Also, a gradual dismissal of transmissionist approaches to favour collaborative approaches involving informed group work and student-centred learning (Kiraly and González Davies 2006: 82).

Relevant in this new pedagogical setting are both aptitude and attitude, mainly related to research on translation strategies and cultural studies, where we can bring together a study of the hidden agenda behind the transference process and final product. A tension between one-to-one renderings and free or emancipatory strategies are at the core of this process where the source text is re-created. Clear examples to present in educational contexts are loaded retellings such as Finn Garner's *Politically Correct Bedtime Stories*, where patriarchal and other conservative values are consciously reversed. Our main question now is: (how) can these reflections and skills be used to improve our understanding of fairy tale retellings? Can procedures be designed to bridge both fields?

Rethinking teaching procedures: projects and other procedures

A project here is defined as a multicompetence assignment that enables the students to engage in professional and pedagogic procedures while they work together towards a tangible end product. There are authentic projects or simulations, depending on whether they have been commissioned by real life needs or initiators, or on whether they mirror these professional assignments or provide practice of the skills necessary for the students to be competent. They can be carried out at any educational level, are usually long term, and involve negotiating with students. They belong mainly to the humanistic and socioconstructivist pedagogical approaches, which are student-centred and forefront holistic creative and critical thinking.

Designing the project: Cinderella, an intercultural and intergenerational study

In our case, the project is authentic in the sense that the activities proposed by the students were to be carried out in their elementary education practice schools. It is also ecological, as its aims coincide with those stated in the general subject syllabus.

The story of Cinderella[4] was chosen because it is well-known and can be traced back for centuries in most cultures in one shape or another. Following group and class discussions, the students agreed to take Disney's version as the leading source text because it is known in most cultures nowadays due to globalising marketing strategies, and because it can be exploited both verbally and visually, as the film is easily available.

Steps

The project consisted of four main parts:

a. Technical features of the selected stories.
b. A description of the heroine's quest in each tale.
c. A comparative study of the renderings based on Translation Studies proposals: degrees of proximity and the transference of cultural references.
d. Classroom procedures for elementary schools (in our setting, for the subject *Learning English as a Foreign Language*).

Improving research skills

Each group of students had to find at least three versions of the story, either in their original language or in English. The teacher guided, but did not give any concrete references. Previous steps were to pool their knowledge about the story, and about fairy tales and relevant websites; to set up an e-list to share any further information; and to set meetings to discuss their progress with other groups.

Applying Translation analysis tools to fairy tale retellings

Hervey, Higgins and Haywood's cline for degrees of fidelity (1995: 13-14) is a good starting point for discussions about similarities and differences in our case. Here follow some examples of the students' adaptation:

Degree of proximity	Verbal elements	Visual elements
Literal: very close to the source contents	*Common elements*: the stepmother and the stepsisters mistreat Cinderella; a slipper or shoe is lost at a party; the Prince/King wants to marry the owner of the shoe; there appears a protector...	(Egyptian) slippers: **Fig. 9-1.** Illustration from *The Wonders of Egypt*. © Reproduced with permission of Thinkquest.

Idiomatic: the extratextual elements have been adapted to the target community without changing the source contents	*Chinese*: a wise old man tells her to kneel before the bones and tell them of her heart's desires – The slippers were woven of golden threads in a pattern of a scaled fish and the soles were made of solid gold...	 **Fig. 9-2.** *La gatta Cenerentola*, Zezolla, a Neapolitan Cinderella, from the website *Parole d'autore*.

Free: the source message and effect, have been adapted to the target community and, so, can present quite a few changes	*Egyptian*: A girl is kidnapped from Greece *Chinese*: the only friend she had was a beautiful fish with big golden eyes - Her stepmother, hearing about the fish, disguised herself as Yen-Shen and enticed the fish from the water. She stabbed it with a dagger, and cooked the fish for dinner. Yeh-Shen was distraught when she learned of the fish's death - the stepmother and daughter were never allowed to visit Yeh-Shen and were forced to continue to live in their cave until the day they were crushed to death in a shower of flying stones

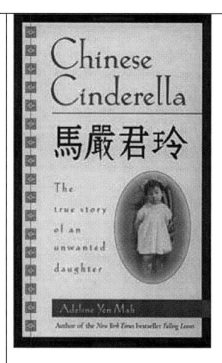

Fig. 9-3. Cover illustration from *Yeh-Shen, A Cinderella Story from China* by Ai-Ling Louie, illustrated by Ed Young © 1982 by Ed Young, illustrations. Used by permission of Philomel Books. All rights reserved.

More specifically, to observe the cultural changes in the different renderings can help develop intercultural awareness and understanding. Cultural references are defined here as:

> Any kind of expression (textual, verbal, non-verbal or audiovisual) denoting any material, ecological, social, religious or linguistic manifestation that can be attributed to a particular community (geographic, socio-economic, professional, linguistic, religious, etc.) and would be admitted as a trait of that community by those who consider themselves to be members of it. (González Davies and Scott-Tennent 2005).

A main point of interest in our case is the choice between cultural transplantation or exotizing strategies[5] that is, in the first case, the text is adapted to the target readers' culture and time whereas in the second case, the translated text keeps the source culture's "foreign" flavour, thus highlighting the differences so that we can learn about the other culture.

To explore both verbal and visual intercultural variations, the cline proposed by Henvey, Higgins and Haywood (1995: 20) was adapted:

Transference Strategy	Verbal elements	Visual elements
Exoticism: The source contents are kept with no changes in the target culture	The versions studied changed the cultural elements to some degree.	North American cultural references known in most countries: globalising versions, such as Disney's.
Communicative translation: The source contents have been slightly adapted to the target culture	The meaning of her name, related to the phoenix, the bird that resurrects from its own ashes (cinders), is adapted: La gatta Cenerentola, Cendrillon, Cenicienta...	*Egyptian*: The god Horus flew down from the sky and took her slipper: **Fig. 9- 4.** Illustration from *The Wonders of Egypt* website. © Reproduced with permission of Thinkquest.

Cultural transplantation: the source contents have been adapted to the target culture	Other names are adopted: *Egyptian*: Rodopis (rosy-cheeked), *Catalan*: Ventafocs (fireplace-cleaner) and Poncellina (bunch of flowers)...	Catalan religious context - The Virgin Mary appears in the sky:  **Fig. 9-5.** Illustration from *La Ventafocs* by Josep Ma. Folch i Torres and Joan Junceda. © Editorial Joventut. Reproduced with permission of Editorial Joventut.

Both clines can be related to research that has been carried out in Translation Studies concerned with what goes on in the translators' minds when carrying out their task and to the knowledge they need to translate professionally. These skills have to do with translation proper and involve problem-spotting and solving, deciding, mental agility, flexibility, adaptability, and resourcing skills, among others.

Activities for elementary schools

Some activities proposed by the participants in the project to carry out with their elementary school students:

Where am I from? Different illustrations from different versions of the story are shown. The students guess their country of origin and other points of interest.

Let's learn new languages! By accessing the following webpages (or any others they may find themselves), the students have the chance to write their names using Chinese and Egyptian hieroglyphics: (http://www.eyelid.co.uk/hiero1.htm; http://www.formosa-translation.com/chinese/).

Travelling around the world! The aim is to relate images and different texts from the versions thay have worked with by giving them maps on which they can stick texts and images they find or create themselves.

Intercultural exhibition: The students and the teacher find out whether there is any cultural event related to fairy tales in their town that school year. Also, the teacher can ask the students to look for different fairy tale images from different countries or to ask their relatives for any they may have (comics, magazines, books or the Internet). Then they can share and discover the different drawings by organising a class or school exhibition. The students can look for fairy tale references in films, ads, etc that school year and add them to their exhibition.

There are many other projects that can be carried out with adult learners: from translating web pages related to the topic to translating a story using different cultural transference strategies (e.g. half the class applies cultural transplantation to the text while the other half applies exotizing strategies). They can send their translations to other classes or to other universities or schools so that they are evaluated by real readers (González Davies 2004), and so on.

Conclusions

Theoretical approaches and observational tools taken from Translation Studies were perceived as an effective means to analyze the retellings. They helped to move away from conventional definitions of fairy tales and of translation towards an open definition more in accordance with recent research in both fields of study.

The formal verbal elements were more evasive in the comparative analysis, as we were dealing with retellings. More work has to be done to design an appropriate tool.

From the pedagogical view, merging both fields helped raise an awareness of intercultural competence and develop critical and creative thinking skills. The project can be adapted and carried out in different subjects at different educational levels. It was specially revealing to concentrate on the divergent verbal and the visual elements to (re)create the emotional impact of the first listening or reading.

New intertextualities recurrently permeate children's, young adults' and adults' literature. In a globalized world used to Disney's prettified Cinderella, to reveal other Cinderellas can be, at the very least, enlightening; in Tymoczko's words: "retranslation and the rewriting of history are one ... Translation acts to counter the petrification of images of the past, of readings of culture and tradition" (2000: 43).

Works Cited

Barthes, Roland, trans. Stephen Heath. "The Death of the Author" In *Image, Music, Text*. London: Fontana Communication Series, 1977.

Basile, Giambattista (1634), *La gatta Cenerentola*. http://www.paroledautore.net/fiabe/classiche/basile/gattacenerentola.htm

Chinese story: Louie, Aai-Ling. *Yeh-Shen, A Cinderella Story*, NY: Philomel Books, 1990. http://www.unc.edu/~rwilkers/resource-china.htm

Egyptian story: from the website *The Wonders of Egypt*. http://library.thinkquest.org/J002037F/egyptian_cinderella.htm

European Commission's Action Plan for Language Learning and Linguistic Diversity, 2005. http://ec.europa.eu/education/policies/lang/policy/index_en.html

Even-Zohar, Itamar. *Polysystem Studies*. Tel Aviv: The Porter Institute for Poetics and Semiotics, 1990.

Folch i Torres, Josep, illus. Joan Junceda. *La Ventafocs. Conte meravellós*. Barcelona: Editorial Mentora/Joventut, 1920.

González Davies, Maria and Christopher Scott-Tennent. "A problem-solving and student-centred approach to the translation of cultural references" In *Meta* (50-1). March. Monograph: *Enseignement de la traduction dans le monde* (2005): 160-179.

González Davies, Maria. *Multiple Voices in the Translation Classroom. Activities, Tasks and Projects*. Amsterdam & Philadelphia: John Benjamins, 2004.

—. "Translation in FLA: Why the Bad Press? A natural activity in an increasingly bilingual world" In *Humanising Language Teaching*, University of Kent: Pilgrims. www.hltmag.co.uk, March, 2007.

Hervey, Sandor, Ian Higgins and Louise Haywood. *Thinking Spanish Translation*, London & New York: Routledge, 1995. (Also, French, Italian, German Translation in the same series).

House, Juliane. "What is an 'Intercultural Speaker'?" In *Intercultural Language Use and Language Learning*, edited by Alcón Soler, E. and M. P. Safont Jordà. Berlin: Springer, (2007): 7-21.

Jakobson, Roman. "On linguistic aspects of translation" In *Selected Writings II: Word and Language*, edited by Jakobson, R. The Hague and Paris: Mouton, (1959/1971): 260-266.

Joosen, Vanessa. "Fairy Tale Retellings between Art and Pedagogy" In *Children's Literature in Education*, vol. 36, no. 2, June, (2005): 129-139.

Kiraly, Don and Maria. "Translation: Pedagogy" In *Elsevier Encyclopaedia of Translation Studies*, 2nd edition, edited by Keith Brown (2006): 81-84.

Macaro, Ernesto. Teaching and Learning a Second Language. A Guide to Recent Research and its Applications. New York: Continuum, 2003/2005.

Nord, Christiane. *Translating as a Purposeful Activity*. Manchester: St. Jerome, 1997.

Nouss, Alexis. "In Praise of Betrayal (On Re-reading Berman), *The Translator* 7: 2.

Toury, Gideon. *Descriptive Translation Studies and Beyond*. Amsterdam-Philadelphia: John Benjamins, 1995.

Tymoczko, Maria. "Translation and Political Engagement. Activism, Social Change and the Role of Translation in Geopolitical Shifts", *The Translator* 6, (2000): 23-47.

Venuti, Lawrence. *The Translator's Invisibility*. London & New York: Routledge, 1995.

Walt Disney Company. *Cinderella*, 1949.

Notes

[1] Also relevant here is the notion of intercultural speaker in foreign language acquisition, which is gradually gaining ground (see, e.g. González Davies 2007, House 2007, Macaro 2003/2005).

[2] The European Union, e.g., explicitly makes reference to the need to include and promote it in educational syllabi (2005): "Policies and Practices for Teaching Socio-cultural Diversity".

[3] Leaving aside the generally accepted distinction between folk and fairy tales, namely, that the former belong to oral tradition and the latter have a known author, I will use the term "fairy tale" here because, with retellings, the existence of a prototypical source text is implicit.

[4] Here, suggestions for the pedagogical applications of Cinderella are presented. In a forthcoming article with Riitta Oittinen, other aspects will be discussed.

---

[5] Venuti deals with domestication and foreignisation strategies from a macrotextual and political point of view, whereas the cultural transposition strategies put forward by Hervey Higgins and Haywood refer to microtextual renderings.

CONTRIBUTORS

Jaqueline S. Du Toit is associate professor in the Department of Afroasiatic Studies, Sign Language and Language Practice. She is a South African National Research Foundation grant holder for women-in-research. Du Toit specializes in the translation of the interface between the visual and oral in religious children's literature, with a special interest in South African children's literature. She has published on this in *Meta*, and in the Journal for Semitics and Old Testament Essays. DuToitJS.HUM@ufs.ac.za

Neus Español studied English Philology and received an MA in Translation from the University of Barcelona, Spain. Her project dealt with the translation into Spanish of the children's book *The Lady in the Box*, by Ann McGovern. She completed this research including a new suggested translation into Spanish, and adding a translation of the book into Catalan. She works as a freelance translator and proofreader, and teaches English and Spanish in the Netherlands. neusescas@chello.nl

Martin B. Fischer studied French, Spanish and Art History at the Freie Universität Berlin. His PhD thesis is *Konrad und Gurkenkönig jenseits der Pyrenäen* (Peter Lang, 2006). Since 1995 he works at the Translation Department of Universitat Pompeu Fabra, Barcelona. He is a professional translator from Catalan, Spanish, French and Dutch into German, and has contributed to several teaching methods of German and Spanish as foreign languages. martin.fischer@upf.edu

Maria González Davies PhD was Head of the Translation Department at the University of Vic and is now a lecturer at the Modern Languages Department of the Faculty of Education at the University Ramon Llull in Barcelona, Spain. Her main research interests are translation training, the role of the L1 and translation in foreign language learning, and young readers' literature in translation. Her publications include articles and books on these topics. mariagd@blanquerna.url.edu

Margherita Ippolito received her PhD in Translation Studies from the University of Bari, Italy. Her dissertation dealt with the specific problems posed by the translation of children's literature. She has written numerous articles on the translation of children's literature. She is part-time lecturer in English Language at the Faculty of Engineering, Polytechnic of Bari, and teaches English and other disciplines in a primary school. margheritaippolito@yahoo.it

At Lamprecht is senior lecturer in Biblical Hebrew and Biblical Aramaic, Faculty of Theology, North-West University, Potchefstroom, South Africa. He specialises in research on Spatial Cognition and Language Use in the Hebrew Bible, the Visual in Bible Translation, and Semitic Philology. His publications include Verb Movement in Biblical Aramaic. *Acta Academica Supplementum* (2001) and The setting of the makkeph in an idea cluster: On homonymy and metonymy, *JNSL 31/2* :107-127, 2005. at.lamprecht@nwu.ac.za

Riitta Oittinen PhD is adjunct professor at the Universities of Helsinki and Tampere and senior lecturer at the University of Tampere, as well as a writer and illustrator. She is also the author of more than 200 publications (books, articles, translations, films, illustrations) and specializes in translating picturebooks and children's literature, especially the verbal, the visual and the auditive (reading aloud). riitta.oittinen@uta.fi

Miquel Pujol Tubau is currently a lecturer in Translation Studies at the University of Vic, Spain. He has carried out research on audiovisual translation and intercultural competence. At the moment, he is working on the contribution to a book to be published about Harry Potter translations into the official languages of Spain. miquelpt@yahoo.com

Salvador Simó i Algado is a lecturer of Occupational Therapy at the University of Vic, Spain. He is the cofounder of the NGO Occupational Theapy without Borders and co-author of *Occupational Therapy without Borders: Learning from the Spirit of Survivors*, (Elsevier, 2005). salvador.simo@uvic.cat

INDEX